BOB CHIEGER

A Fireside Book
PUBLISHED BY
SIMON & SCHUSTER INC.
NEW YORK   LONDON

FOOTBALL'S GREATEST QUOTES

AND PAT SULLIVAN

TORONTO   SYDNEY   TOKYO   SINGAPORE

Books by Bob Chieger

Voices of Baseball
Inside Golf (with Pat Sullivan)
The Cubbies

Books by Pat Sullivan

Inside Golf (with Bob Chieger)

FIRESIDE
Simon & Schuster Building
Rockefeller Center
1230 Avenue of the Americas
New York, New York 10020

FIRESIDE and colophon are registered trademarks
of Simon & Schuster Inc.

Designed by Glen M. Edelstein
Manufactured in the United States of America

1 2 3 4 5 6 7 8 9 10 Pbk.

Library of Congress Cataloging in Publication Data

Chieger, Bob.
Football's greatest quotes / Bob Chieger and Pat Sullivan.
p.   cm.
"A Fireside book."
Includes bibliographical references (p.   ) and index.
1. Football—United States—Quotations, maxims, etc.
I. Sullivan, Pat.   II. title.
GV959.C45 1990   90-41859
796.332'0973—dc20   CIP

ISBN 0-671-69368-9 Pbk.

CONTENTS

INTRODUCTION 7
Bowl Games 11
Brains and Flakes 14
Chalkboard 20
Character 24
Cheerleaders 28
Coaching 30
Coaches: The Colleges 34
Coaches: The Pros 39
College Football 50
Colleges and Universities 56
Defensive Backs 71
Defensive Linemen 74
Diet and Exercise 81
Equipment 83
Famous Last Words 87
Fans and Alumni 92
Football: The Game 96
Football and Other Activities 101
Great Rivalries 104
Heavy Hitting 106
High Times 109
Labor 113
Linebackers 116

Modern Days/Olden Days 124
Monday Night Football 127
Money 130
NFL Teams 132
Offensive Linemen 151
On the Road 159
Owners and Executives 161
Pain and Injury 166
Pass Receivers 170
Pep Talk 174
Philosophy 179
Pro Leagues 183
Quarterbacks 187
Recruiting and Drafting 203
Retirement 206
Running Backs 209
Special Teams 221
Sportswriters 224
Super Bowl 227
Television and Radio 236
Training Camp 240
Win, Lose, and Tie 243
Women 248
Bibliography 255
Index 261

INTRODUCTION

"Nothing is better in this world than driving to Ann Arbor or East Lansing on a crisp Saturday morning for a football game," wrote *Detroit Free Press* columnist Joe Falls.

Since I grew up in Detroit, this quote reminds me of those glorious bronze fall mornings in southern Michigan when Dad and I would wake up knowing we could skip the weekly lawn mowing, car washing, or grocery shopping. On those football Saturdays, we'd get to explore the city surrounding the University of Michigan or stroll the well-trimmed campus of Michigan State.

September. We'd walk down paths cut through broad, well-cut lawns, looking up at the buildings or at sharply dressed coeds in plaid skirts, reddened knees showing off the last of their summer tans. Dad and I would look at each other now and then and smile, anticipating the colorful football spectacle ahead.

For us, football brought us days outside experiencing the fresh autumn air. We breathed it in, and always felt wonderful.

In October, when the first cold snap jolted our fall reverie, the morning sky now a steel-gray, we would spend a Sunday morning getting the mittens and mufflers out of the attic. We'd bundle up and enjoy the chill air watching the Detroit Lions with friends, family, and neighboring fans. In this book, broadcaster Pat Summerall is kidded for crying at a football game on Thanksgiving Day. I cry when I hear the bars of the Lions' theme song, played in a minor key. November is a tough month, but the songs of football are within us.

In December, when cold rain slanted against the picture

window or snow began softly falling at dusk, we would gather in front of the television set to enjoy a game.

January brought the holiday bowl games and later, the Super Bowl, a national holiday in a month that really needed one.

I enjoy football because it brings us together; it tells us that we can survive whatever winter brings us.

For this book, Pat Sullivan and I have collected the quotes, humorous and profound, of America's game. We surveyed the football literature, hoping to catch the flavor of the game in the words of the players, coaches, and fans, adding quotes from radio, television, magazines, and newspapers.

Football fans have always known that the game has its characters—the equal of any other sport. It's a team game, yes, but how do you explain the many unforgettable individuals: Bum Phillips, Bobby Layne, Alex Karras, Lyle Alzado, John Madden, Ken Stabler, to name but a few. We have tried to capture their personalities here.

This book was put together by football fans for football fans. We hope you take it with you to share with friends during time-outs and at halftime, or sit by the fire on a winter evening.

We'd like to thank those who made this book possible. We both owe a great deal to our agent Kathi Paton and editor Ed Walters. Pat would like to thank friends Ed and Bob Burns, Stan Hochman, Al Moss, Eugene Lesser and Lee Grosscup, and especially Larry Sullivan, Jim Sullivan and Mike Sullivan, for throwing spirals on Thanksgiving afternoons. I owe it all to my folks, Dan and Deloris Chieger, and to the Mayos—Hank, Mary, and Steve—for their generosity and caring.

Bob Chieger
Portland, Oregon
June 1990

You know, it's a pretty weird game when you think about it.

Clare Farnsworth, football writer,
quoted in Fred Moody,
*Fighting Chance: An NFL Season
with the Seattle Seahawks,* 1989

Boys, don't be nervous. There are only going to be thirty million people watching us.

> Pete Elliott, California coach, prior to the Rose Bowl, 1959

I remember it was a beautiful day because I spent most of it lying on my back looking up at the blue sky.

> Joe Kapp, California quarterback, on a 38–12 loss to Iowa in the Rose Bowl, 1959

I've been to the Fiesta Bowl for the past two years. It will certainly be nice to take the team with me.

> LaVell Edwards, Brigham Young coach, 1974

Every year we keep going to a minor bowl. If they have a Soybean Bowl next year, we'll probably be at that.

> Jack Staples, Louisiana State board of supervisors

The thing is that 90 percent of the colleges are abiding by the rules, doing things right. The other 10 percent, they're going to the bowl games.

> Tony Mason, University of Cincinnati coach
> *Sports Illustrated*, 1975

When I took this job I promised our fans I'd show them a Rose Bowl team.

Lee Corso, Indiana coach, before
facing Southern Cal in the Rose Bowl
Sports Illustrated, 1981

If a [television] network wanted to move the Rose Bowl or the Cotton Bowl to Buenos Aires, universities' secretaries would be dialing directory assistance for Argentine Airlines.

Mike Downey, sports columnist
Chicago Sun-Times, 1981

We'll have parity if Vanderbilt represents the SEC in the Sugar Bowl and Northwestern plays Oregon State in the Rose Bowl. But the Second Coming or Armageddon will happen before that.

Beano Cook, football analyst
Inside Sports, 1982

If you are 10–1, you go to a major bowl; 9–2, you go somewhere; 8–3, it is shaky; and 7–4, it is Christmas in New England.

Jack Bicknell, Boston College coach
USA Today, 1983

I know why we lost the Civil War. We must have had the same officials.

Bum Phillips, Saints coach, when his
South team lost the Senior Bowl
The Sporting News, 1983

The Pro Bowl became the Rodney Dangerfield of all-star games. . . . It was the only game that Will Rogers couldn't like. The mutual fund that E. F. Hutton couldn't sell. Norman Vincent Peale couldn't find a positive aspect to the thing.

Tom Barnidge, sports editor
The Sporting News, 1983

Just make the Pro Bowl a golf tournament in midseason, with each player wearing his team's helmet on the course.

> Dan Dierdorf, Cardinals center
> *The Sporting News*, 1983

Last year we got official Holiday Bowl watches. This year the bowl has offered to fix the official Holiday Bowl watches.

> Glen Kozlowski, Brigham Young
> receiver
> *USA Today*, 1984

It's the first bowl I've ever seen that I don't have to clean.

> Erma Bombeck, columnist, grand
> marshal of the Tournament of Roses
> Parade
> *Newsweek*, 1986

The Iowa football team will visit Disneyland today. If there is a betting line, take the mouse.

> Art Thiel, sportswriter, after Iowa lost
> 45–28 to UCLA in the Rose Bowl
> *Seattle Post-Intelligencer*, 1986

What the iceberg was to the *Titanic,* what Little Big Horn was to Custer, Waterloo to Napoleon, Tunney to Dempsey, the Rose Bowl is to Bo Schembechler.

> Jim Murray, sports columnist, on the
> Michigan coach's 1–8 record in
> Pasadena
> *Los Angeles Times*, 1988

A Freedom Bowl is (choose one):

1. A football game played annually in Shreveport—or, possibly, Memphis.
2. The tabloid name given to what's happening in eastern Europe today.
3. A new 32-lane facility in Downey where the last 300 game was rolled.

4. A place where you go to watch the Easter sunrise ser-
vices.

> Jim Murray, sports columnist
> *Los Angeles Times,* 1989

BRAINS AND FLAKES

I know the lad you mean. Great big hands. Shoulders a mile
wide. Yeah, that guy doesn't know his own strength, or anything else.

> Knute Rockne, Notre Dame coach,
> on a prospect

It was a terrible boner. I don't know how it happened. I
can't even think of a decent alibi.

> Roy "Wrong Way" Riegels, of
> California, following the Rose Bowl
> game in which he ran the wrong way
> and was tackled on the one-yard line,
> 1929

Springhill, Louisiana, is so far back in the woods they had
to pipe in sunshine.

> John David Crow, running back, on
> his hometown

I could have been a Rhodes scholar except for my grades.

> Duffy Daugherty, Michigan State
> coach

No damn sign is going to tell me what to do.

> Joe Don Looney, Giants rookie
> running back, refusing to throw his
> socks in a marked bin, 1964

I never met a man I didn't like . . . until I met Will Rogers.

> Joe Don Looney

If I was smart enough to be a doctor, I'd be a doctor. I ain't, so I'm a football player.

> Dick Butkus, Illinois linebacker

It was like a heart transplant. We tried to implant college in him, but his head rejected it.

> Barry Switzer, Oklahoma coach, on a
> failed prospect

How do you want to work this, Coach? Want me to go for the win or just tie the game up for you?

> Bobby Douglass, Chargers
> quarterback, entering the game
> trailing 47–17 with three minutes
> left, 1975

If I can ever get my players and coaches to make as few mistakes as the officials, there ain't nobody who's ever going to beat us.

> Red Sanders, UCLA coach

Officials are the only guys who can rob you and then get a police escort out of the stadium.

> Rob Bolton, Browns defensive back
> *Sports Illustrated,* 1978

I may be dumb, but I'm not stupid.

> Terry Bradshaw, Steelers quarterback
> "Thursday Night Edition,"
> ABC-TV, 1980

This isn't nuclear physics. It's a game. How smart do you really have to be?

> Terry Bradshaw
> *The Seattle Times,* 1984

I probably would have ended up as an elegant fop. Maybe I would have learned the harpsichord. At this very moment I might be the Secretary of the Interior, lolling on a sofa in Washington with an ecology student.

> Alex Karras, former Lions defensive tackle, when asked what he would have been if he hadn't gone into sports

The greatest thing I ever did at USC was graduate.

> Tim Rossovich, former defensive lineman and linebacker, on Southern California
> *San Jose Mercury News*, 1980

You can get a reputation as a great cook by perfecting only two or three dishes. Just make sure you keep inviting different people over to eat.

> Chuck Noll, Steelers coach
> *Sports Illustrated*, 1980

When I was with St. Louis, they said it was a Cinderella team. I was at New Orleans and they called it a Cinderella team. Now they're doing it with the Bills. All that talk's okay, but I don't want anyone to get the idea I'm a fairy.

> Conrad Dobler, Bills guard
> *San Jose Mercury News*, 1980

My guidance counselor said to me: "A lot of people in this world don't know what's going on, but Lou Holtz, you don't even *suspect* anything is going on."

> Lou Holtz, Arkansas coach
> "The Tonight Show," NBC-TV, 1981

I've played for guys that didn't know if the ball was pumped or stuffed.

> Lew Erber, Raiders receivers coach
> *San Francisco Chronicle*, 1981

Who was the guy who missed a game because he couldn't find the Superdome? . . . He was a punt returner named Williams, I think. . . . Next day, Coach North said, "Where were you?" Williams said, "Coach, I couldn't find the Superdome." And Coach North said, "Well, I hope you can find the damn airport."

> Archie Manning, Saints quarterback
> *Sports Illustrated*, 1981

Anyone in the NFL who subscribes to *National Geographic* is considered a genius.

> Larry Felser, sports columnist
> *Inside Sports*, 1982

America would be amazed at how few players can carry a play into the game from the sidelines. That's one of the great unknown comedies in the game.

> Ahmad Rashad, Vikings receiver
> *Sports Illustrated*, 1982

Actually, I was only at Iowa two terms—Truman's and Eisenhower's.

> Alex Karras, former Lions defensive
> tackle
> *The Sporting News*, 1983

He [tackle Earl Jones] can move around pretty good. He just didn't move to class too well.

> Bill Yeoman, University of Houston
> coach
> *Sports Illustrated*, 1983

I look a lot faster when I wear 36.

> Glenn Watson, Vanderbilt defensive
> end, changing his number
> from 92
> *The Sporting News*, 1983

From the waist down, Earl Campbell has the biggest legs I've ever seen on a running back.

> John Madden, broadcaster
> "NFL Football," CBS-TV, 1983

I'm starting to understand all the things you say. It scares me a little bit.

> Gary Bender, broadcaster, to Madden
> "NFL Football," CBS-TV, 1981

There were three types of kids: the big fat sissies, the guys with ducktail haircuts and black leather jackets, and the athletes. My hair was too curly for a ducktail, so I had to go with sports. If I'd had straight hair, I might be in prison today.

> John Riggins, Redskins running back
> *Sports Illustrated,* 1983

I spent five years learning to spell Chattanooga, then we moved to Albuquerque.

> Joe Morrison, South Carolina coach
> *Sports Illustrated,* 1983

I don't really trust a sane person. You can never depend on them.

> Lyle Alzado, Raiders defensive
> lineman
> *The Washington Post,* 1984

I've never met a great player who wasn't a little goofy.

> John Madden, CBS-TV broadcaster
> *Hey, Wait a Minute, I Wrote a
> Book!,* 1984

I'm just slow.

> Marty Schottenheimer, Browns
> coach, on why he works eighteen-
> hour days
> *Sports Illustrated,* 1985

There were so many of us that by the time we got finished saying good night, it was morning.

> William Dalton, running back, on his
> twenty brothers and sisters
> *Chicago Sun-Times,* 1985

The problem with having a sense of humor is often that people you use it on aren't in a very good mood.

> Lou Holtz, Notre Dame coach
> *Sports Illustrated,* 1985

I don't know. I'm not from the Lords of London.

> Hank Bullough, Bills coach, when
> asked if a player had insurance
> *San Francisco Chronicle,* 1986

That took the sails out of our wind.

> Hank Bullough, on an opponent's
> ninety-six-yard touchdown pass
> *San Francisco Chronicle,* 1986

If England was so nice, why did everybody leave and come to America?

> Doug Cosbie, Cowboys tight end
> *Sports Illustrated,* 1986

The second-dumbest thing I ever said was when my daughter was born, and I asked the doctor, "Are you sure it's a girl?"

> Randy Cross, 49ers guard
> *The Sporting News,* 1986

I don't need the news. If they have a war, I figure someone will tell me.

> Bum Phillips, former coach
> *Los Angeles Times,* 1986

Enberg: What's your book about?
Carson: About $16.95 at your local bookstore.

> Harry Carson, Giants linebacker, to
> Dick Enberg
> "NFL Football," NBC-TV, 1986

The tests historically discriminate against those not in the mainland or streamlined.

> Jackie Sherrill, Texas A&M coach, on
> SAT tests
> *Sports Illustrated,* 1987

I guess I left him hanging.

> Mark Rypien, who stood up Vice
> President Dan Quayle for dinner, 1989

CHALKBOARD

It starts out like a short sweep, turns into what looks like an end-around play to the long side, and finally winds up with a delayed reverse straight over the spot where the short side defensive end should be, but usually isn't. It's sort of a psychic double-cross.

> Fielding Yost, Michigan coach, on his
> Old 83 play

Tackling is more natural than blocking. If a man is running down the street with everything you own, you won't let him get away. That's tackling.

> Vince Lombardi, Packers coach

It was a twin-two-sweep-trap. That means as much to me as it does to you.

> Joe Don Looney, Colts running back,
> to reporters on scoring a touchdown
> in his first professional game, 1964

Gilmer: If they go into a four-four, tell [quarterback Milt] Plum to use a thirty-three sweep.
Looney: Look, Coach, if you want a messenger, call Western Union.

> Joe Don Looney, Lions running back,
> to coach Harry Gilmer during a
> game, 1965

Gillman, showing films to his assistant: Bum, this is better than making love.
Phillips: Either I don't know how to watch film, or you don't know how to make love.

> Bum Phillips, Chargers defensive
> assistant, to coach Sid Gillman

You've heard about the Rubber Band Defense that bends but never breaks? Ours doesn't break either, but it stretches 101 yards.

> Don Smith, former Giants publicist,
> 1971

I can tell whether a player is on offense or defense just by looking at his locker. The offensive players keep their lockers clean and orderly, but the lockers of the defensive men are a mess. In fact, the better the defensive player, the bigger the mess.

> Arnold J. Mandell, psychiatrist
> *Saturday Review,* 1974

We were tipping off our plays. Whenever we broke from the huddle, three backs were laughing and one was pale as a ghost.

> John Breen, former Oilers general
> manager
> *Sports Illustrated,* 1974

I forgot about the playbook. I forgot about the computer. The formations didn't tell me anything. When they lined up, all I could think about was, "Look how big these sons of bitches are!"

Thomas "Hollywood" Henderson,
Cowboys linebacker, on his first NFL
game, 1975

When you came after us at Pearl Harbor, you were on offense and we were on defense. And when we came after you at Nagasaki, we were on offense and you were on defense.

Conrad Dobler, Cardinals guard,
explaining football to the Japanese,
1976

On the rest of it, just do what you usually do.

Rickey Young, Vikings running back,
forgetting the play he brought in

Football ain't nothing but offenses cooking something up and defenses chasing 'em and catching 'em.

Abe Martin, Texas Christian coach
Sports Illustrated, 1980

I don't want the little play, the average play. I want the *big* play. Hell, I'm not going to stay up all night trying to figure out how to gain three yards.

Sid Gillman, former coach, 1981

On the whole, the pros move the football on the ground as if it were a piano.

John Underwood, sportswriter
Sports Illustrated, 1981

I'd rather pass against a "prevent" defense than a hard rush any time. . . . But I really shouldn't mention this too often, or I might be out of a job.

Brian Sipe, Browns quarterback
San Francisco Examiner, 1981

The offense sells the tickets and the defense wins the games.

> Lindsey Nelson, sportscaster
> "NFL Football," CBS-TV, 1982

That's what I've always loved about football—the human element. The computer charts an "Opposite slot left, Zoom, Fake 36, Z reverse pass left"—and the play works because the safety falls down.

> Pat Haden, former Rams quarterback
> *Sports Illustrated*, 1982

For example, the phrase "Take what the defense gives you." That never made any sense. You know, everyone just kind of nods knowingly, muttering, "Good point, good point." But no one ever says, "Well, what the hell does that mean?"

> John Madden, CBS-TV broadcaster
> *Sport*, 1983

That play looked like a menu in a Chinese restaurant.

> Pat Summerall, sportscaster, on a
> complicated play by Dallas
> "NFL Football," CBS-TV, 1983

Our running game's going to consist of running on the field and running off the field.

> Tom Moore, The Citadel coach
> *Sports Illustrated*, 1983

No, he'll call our plays. We aren't going to let him make up any.

> Bum Phillips, Saints coach, when
> asked if Archie Manning would call
> his own plays
> *USA Today*, 1985

Defense is like a dog. It will mind you. Offense is fickle— like a cat. It won't listen to you. An ol' cat that you tell to go out the door will just sit there, scratching at you.

> Bobby Bowden, Florida State coach
> *Sports Illustrated*, 1985

We will use some kind of option, and we will throw the football. I hope it will be at our people.

> Lou Holtz, University of Minnesota
> coach, 1985

Last year it was run, run, run and punt. Now it will be pass, pass, pass and punt.

> Stan Parrish, Kansas State coach, on
> his new offense, 1986

The most deceptive course in football is straight at the goalposts. When the Germans went through the Argonne, it was not an 18 sweep, it was a 10 trap.

> Woody Hayes, former Ohio State
> coach
> *Sports Illustrated,* 1987

There's nothing wrong with reading the game plan by the light of a jukebox.

> Ken Stabler, former quarterback
> *Dallas Morning News,* 1987

 **CHARACTER**

One man practicing sportsmanship is far better than fifty preaching it.

> Knute Rockne, Notre Dame coach
> *Coaching,* 1925

What is courage? Courage means to be afraid to do something and still going ahead and doing it. If a man has character, the right kind of energy, mental ability, he will learn that fear is something to overcome and not to run away from.

> Knute Rockne, 1931

I've seen moral courage in football as often as physical. I've seen football make men out of condemned material. Football? A great game—a great game.

> John W. Heisman, former coach
> *Collier's*, 1929

If a boy wants to play football and for any reason you keep him from it, you will probably find that his character—or his temper, at least—will not improve.

> Eleanor Roosevelt
> *Ladies' Home Journal*, 1942

How can I win? If I say I'm glad, I'm a traitor, and if I say I'm sorry, I'm a fool.

> Joe Namath, Jets quarterback, on
> flunking his Army physical, 1965

We have to avoid being *nice,* that's all. That's what I tell the boys all the time. It's this *niceness* from people complimenting you that can be killing. It can be deceiving.

> Woody Hayes, Ohio State coach,
> 1968

You give me a good boy, and I'll give you a good boy back.

> Bobby Dodd, Georgia Tech coach, to
> a mother who wanted discipline for
> her son

I personally believe that in life as in football all of us have good field positions.

> Roger Staubach, Cowboys
> quarterback, 1971

Football doesn't build character. It eliminates the weak ones.

> Darrell Royal, Texas coach
> *Sports Illustrated*, 1973

God does not grade on a curve; do right at all times.

Lou Holtz, Arkansas coach

People complain that we are victims of a permissive society. Well, I'll tell you this—we don't have one player on my team who "does his own thing." We aren't permissive here. At Ohio State, they do *our* thing.

Woody Hayes, Ohio State coach

Nothing is work unless you'd rather be doing something else.

George Halas, Bears coach

I've been an optimist since I was a kid. I can still remember the Christmas morning I ran down to my stocking and found it full of horse manure. I yelled, "Hey, I got a pony around here somewhere."

Duffy Daugherty, Michigan State
coach

Two kinds of football players ain't worth a damn. One that never does what he's told, and the other that never does anything *except* what he's told.

Bum Phillips, Oilers coach
He Ain't No Bum, 1979

Being a football player doesn't make me any different than the guy who is out there diggin' ditches and layin' pipe. The way I was raised, if I ever got cocky or started thinkin' I was halfway cool, my old man would hit me in the mouth.

Ken Stabler, Oilers quarterback
San Jose Mercury News, 1980

The road to Easy Street goes through the dump.

John Madden, former Raiders coach,
1980

Man should be completely free of all the little whimsical rules that are thrown at you by society. You should honor polite commitments, but you must be your own man.

> John Matuszak, Raiders defensive
> end
> *Sport,* 1981

People are human. If you're going to criticize them, compliment them first.

> Bum Phillips, Saints coach
> *Playboy,* 1981

I want players to have their habits down so they don't have to think about them. If you have to think about opening your mouth, you won't be a very good eater.

> Bum Phillips
> *Playboy,* 1981

Coming from Greek-Irish-Scottish-Midwestern stock, a man's role was very defined. When you were twenty-one, you got married, had kids, worked hard, and saved money till you were sixty-five. You were a *man,* by God, *strong.* You never showed your feelings and you *never* changed. If you lived long enough, you retired to Florida, sat in a deck chair, and breathed oxygen out of a bottle. But life's not like that. I finally admitted I was resisting change, growth. I realized I never really was the macho cretin that football cast me as, so I stopped playing the role.

> Alex Karras, defensive tackle-turned-
> actor
> *TV Guide,* 1982

You can't make the club in a tub.

> John Ralston, Stanford coach

Pride is hard to swallow, but it will go down.

Conrad Dobler, Bills guard
Dallas Times-Herald, 1982

When I wake up in the morning, the German in me shouts, "*Achtung!* Let's get going!" Then the Mexican in me says, "*Mañana*" . . . and I roll over and go back to sleep.

Joe Kapp, former quarterback
Sports Illustrated, 1982

 **CHEERLEADERS**

The NFL will have to adopt a hands-off policy on cheerleaders.

Pete Rozelle, NFL commissioner

Deep down every cheerleader in school was a closet nymphomaniac. They all wanted to be lustful pervs. Somewhere in the deep reaches of their consciousness they all wanted to go out there and cavort like all the weird people did.

Frank Zappa, musician and composer

They're taking over the game. They've got locker rooms, draft choices, and everything. Mary Sue there probably went in the first round. Good hands.

John Madden, CBS-TV broadcaster
Sports Illustrated, 1980

Harmon: What do you get out of working with the Raiders?
LoCosale: A Raiderette.

Al LoCosale, Raiders executive, to
broadcaster Tom Harmon, 1981

These are the girl-next-door types, if you happen to live next door to Caesars Palace.

> Bob Costas, sportscaster, on the
> Cincinnati Ben-Gals cheerleaders
> "NFL Football," NBC-TV, 1982

I played there [Dallas] when I was with the Bears. I borrowed Roger Stillwell's helmet on the sidelines. Biggest hat on the team, size eight. I took out the cheek pads so it would swivel freely on my head, and I turned it around so the face bar was facing the field, and I turned my head and watched the cheerleaders through the earhole.

> Mike Adamle, former Bears halfback
> *Sports Illustrated,* 1982

Where little girls used to dream of being Miss America, now they dream of becoming a cheerleader for the Cowboys instead.

> Suzanne Mitchell, Dallas Cowboys
> Cheerleaders executive
> *Sports Illustrated,* 1982

Whether you like this kind of *shtick* or loathe it, you must admit that the sight of a Dallas Cowboys cheerleader shimmying in the Texas moonlight is one of the great byproducts of the Industrial Age.

> Dick Friedman, journalist
> *TV Guide,* 1983

When you stare at the Dallas cowgirls you're not staring at talent. You look at most of the moves, the gyration, the twisting, what they wear, it's really a sexual symbolism. Anybody who sees no relation to sex is either blind, deaf and dumb, or all of them.

> Thomas Tutko, psychology professor
> *USA Today,* 1983

To sing like Barbra Streisand, dance like Juliet Prowse, and possess the wit of Kermit the Frog.

> Julee Graham, Dallas Cowboys
> cheerleader, on the qualities she
> would like to have
> *USA Today,* 1984

There just aren't enough good-looking girls in Green Bay for the Dallas Cowboy cheerleader look.

> Max McGee, former Packers receiver
> *Sports Illustrated,* 1984

 **COACHING**

It's a lot tougher to be a football coach than a president. You've got four years as president, and they guard you. A coach doesn't have anyone to protect him when things go wrong.

> Harry S Truman
> *Sports Illustrated,* 1958

A successful coach is one who is still coaching.

> Ben Schwartzwalder, Syracuse coach,
> 1963

My mama wanted me to be a preacher. I told her coachin' and preachin' were a lot alike. I don't think she believed me.

> Bear Bryant, Alabama coach

A head coach is guided by this main objective: dig, claw, wheedle, coach that fanatical effort out of the players. You want them to play every Saturday as if they were planting the flag on Iwo Jima.

> Darrell Royal, Texas coach
> *Darrell Royal Talks Football,* 1963

A coach likes to have a lot of those old trained pigs who'll grin and jump right in the slop for him.

Darrell Royal

If you really want to advise me, do it on Saturday afternoon between one and four o'clock. And you've got twenty-five seconds to do it, between plays. Not on Monday. I know the right thing to do on Monday.

Alex Agase, Purdue coach

They give you a Cadillac one year, and the next year they give you the gas to get out of town.

Woody Hayes, Ohio State coach

I have been asked to speak at everything but a Bar Mitzvah. I always say I'm going to talk about sex and marriage, but being a football coach's wife, I don't know anything about either.

Anne Hayes, wife of Woody

Coaches! You hire them and you give them the players, and once they win, you can't tell them anything.

Carroll Rosenbloom, Rams owner
San Francisco Chronicle, 1979

If my daddy worked at a regular job as much as he does at football, we'd be millionaires.

Mike Perkins, age eleven, son of
Giants coach Ray Perkins
San Francisco Examiner, 1979

There are two types of coaches: them that have just been fired, and them that are going to be fired.

Bum Phillips
Playboy, 1981

Perhaps the only job as insecure as coaching in the NFL is capping oil well fires.

Thomas Boswell, sportswriter
The Washington Post, 1981

If you want to drop off the face of the earth, just be an assistant coach.

> Bob Griese, former Dolphins
> quarterback
> *Dallas Times-Herald,* 1982

Coaches are always up for meetings.

> Ahmad Rashad, Vikings receiver
> *Sports Illustrated,* 1982

I have to talk to the press after games. I thought that's what coaches are for.

> John Elway, Stanford quarterback,
> 1982

Dan Reeves . . . looked like a man who had turned on his sprinkler and found it was spewing oil.

> Douglas S. Looney, sportswriter, on
> the Broncos coach after John Elway
> led Denver to a seventy-five-yard
> winning touchdown in his first game
> *Sports Illustrated,* 1983

My dog was about my only friend, and I told my wife that man needs at least two friends. She bought me another dog.

> Pepper Rodgers, recalling a bad year
> coaching at UCLA
> *San Francisco Examiner,* 1983

There are four things people are experts on: religion, politics, sex, and coaching football.

> Ray Alborn, Rice coach
> *Inside Sports,* 1983

Most coaches, it turns out, were mediocre college players if they played in college at all. A lot of them lost their taste for hitting after they got out of high school and found themselves on a field where everybody could hit back. And for a lot of them, their senior year in high school was as good as it ever got . . . . They had coaches then who told them it would last forever, and advised them to put off the girls till later. The ones who believed that became coaches themselves.

> Pete Dexter, journalist
> *Esquire,* 1983

Tom Landry told me it's not that hard to become a great football coach. He said it's all in how you wear the hat.

> Gary Busey, actor, preparing to play
> the late Bear Bryant in the film *Bear*
> *The Sporting News,* 1983

I saw the Bear play the Bear.

> Bum Phillips, former Bryant assistant
> at Texas A&M, with no plans to see
> the movie
> *Sports Illustrated,* 1984

I don't know enough to coach an extra day.

> Dick Coury, New Orleans Breakers
> coach, on why he gave his team an
> extra day off before a Monday night
> game, 1984

Every coach is in the last year of his contract. Some just don't know it.

> Dan Henning, Falcons coach, 1985

A wit once defined college coaches as "a class of selfless sufferers who go on building character year after year, no matter how many states they have to import it from."

> George F. Will, writer
> *Newsweek,* 1986

Humility is only seven days away.

> Barry Switzer, Oklahoma coach
> *Time,* 1986

In the language of football, "resign" is a code word meaning "he was given the choice of quitting, being fired, or having the fans blow up his house."

> Gene Klein, former Chargers owner
> *First Down and a Billion*, 1987

You know what NFL stands for? Not For Long.

> Jerry Glanville, Oilers coach
> *Sports Illustrated*, 1989

 **COACHES: THE COLLEGES**

BEAR BRYANT—Maryland, Kentucky, and Alabama 1945–1982

The Bear's always been ahead of us humans. Even when we started the two-platoon system, he was using three platoons: one on offense, one on defense, and one to go to class.

> Frank Howard, Clemson coach

When you scrape away all the hayseed, you find you're looking at the Royal Flush underneath. You can beat the Bear once, but never the same way twice.

> John McKay, Southern California
> coach

I thought to myself, "This is what God must look like."

> George Blanda, quarterback, on first
> meeting Bryant at Kentucky in 1946
> *Southern Living*, 1981

Bryant's face is brown and as rutted as the erosion of a dried-up riverbed. Under his Henry Higgins hat, the fire in his eyes could burn a hole in a vault. The twinkle in them can melt a [recruit's] mother's heart.

> Tom Callahan, sportswriter
> *Time,* 1982

The only guy I don't want to run against in Alabama is Bear Bryant.

> George Wallace, governor of Alabama
> "NBC Nightly News," NBC-TV, 1982

BOB DEVANEY—WYOMING AND NEBRASKA 1957–1973

I remember following two guys into a Nebraska game on a rainy day. One turned to the other and said, "It wouldn't be raining if Devaney were still coaching."

> Deloss Dodds, Texas athletic director
> *Sports Illustrated,* 1986

GERRY FAUST—NOTRE DAME 1981–1985

We're behind Gerry all the way for the time being.

> Walt Egierski, South Bend
> sheet-metal worker
> *Newsweek,* 1981

If handed a bushel of thorns, [Faust] would start looking for the roses.

> Douglas S. Looney, sportswriter
> *Sports Illustrated,* 1983

DANNY FORD—CLEMSON 1978–1989

He don't use good English. He chews tobacco. He don't play golf. He drives a pickup truck, and he don't play the stock market. What's *not* to love about him?

> Jimmy Howard, Clemson,
> South Carolina, tavern owner
> *Atlanta Constitution,* 1987

WOODY HAYES—Denison, Miami (Ohio), and Ohio State 1946–1978

If he thought it might rain on Saturday, he would hold practices in the rain. If he thought it might be muddy on Saturday, he would hold practices in the mud. If he felt it might snow on Saturday, he would order a practice blizzard down from the Lord on Wednesday.

> Dan Jenkins, sportswriter
> *Sports Illustrated*, 1968

His closest associate was a blackboard with circles and x's on it, or a film projector.

> Dan Jenkins
> *Sports Illustrated*, 1968

I've hated him for years. We've had a wonderful relationship.

> Joe Falls, sports columnist
> *Detroit Free Press*, 1971

In politics and philosophy he ranges somewhere to the right of Calvin Coolidge, Pat Boone, Richard Nixon, and Friedrich Nietzsche.

> Jerry Brondfield, writer and editor
> *Woody Hayes and the 100-Yard War*,
> 1974

Woody passes up more opportunities to keep his mouth shut in one year than most people do in a lifetime.

> Mervin D. Hyman and Gordon S.
> White, Jr., sportswriters
> *Big Ten Football*, 1977

Woody was consistent. Graceless in victory and graceless in defeat.

> Jim Murray, sports columnist

LOU HOLTZ—WILLIAM AND MARY, NORTH CAROLINA STATE, NEW YORK JETS, ARKANSAS, MINNESOTA, AND NOTRE DAME 1969–

Holtz is a kind of combination snake-oil salesman, evangelist, and hard-nosed business executive. That means he is constantly talking out of both sides of his mouth.

> Douglas S. Looney, sportswriter
> *Sports Illustrated*, 1986

Lou Holtz can talk faster than I can listen.

> Fred Akers, Texas coach

JIMMY JOHNSON—MIAMI 1984–1988

The only time Jimmy didn't run up a score was twenty-seven years ago when he took the SAT.

> Jim Nantz, CBS-TV broadcaster
> *Sports Illustrated*, 1988

JOHNNY MAJORS—IOWA STATE, PITTSBURGH, AND TENNESSEE 1968–

I couldn't understand a word Coach Majors said, but I sure liked the way he said it.

> Tony Dorsett, on his recruitment for
> the University of Pittsburgh
> *Sports Illustrated*, 1979

JOHN McKAY—SOUTHERN CALIFORNIA 1960–1975

Some of the stuff he suggested was too far out for us at Oregon. We had to reject some of his plays because we would have needed motorcycles to make them work.

> Len Casanova, Oregon coach, on
> McKay as an assistant

Anybody that's met John McKay knows you don't have to be around him very long before you want to beat his ass.

Jim Finks, Bears general manager
Sport, 1982

KNUTE ROCKNE—NOTRE DAME 1918–1930

You died one of our national heroes. Notre Dame was your address, but every gridiron in America was your home.

Will Rogers, eulogy, 1931

He was a daddy to us all. We even went to him if we fell in love with a new girl.

Elmer Layden, former Notre Dame
fullback, 1931

Rockne wanted nothing but "bad losers." Good losers get into the habit of losing. Rockne wanted boys who would tear their hair out by the handfuls on the rare occasions when Notre Dame lost.

George E. Allen, writer
Presidents Who Have Known Me,
1950

JIM SHOFNER—TEXAS CHRISTIAN 1974–1976

He's such a nice guy. But if they had a Naive Bowl, he'd coach both sides.

Orville Henry, sportswriter

BARRY SWITZER—OKLAHOMA 1971–1988

When he wants to be charming, as when he's in pursuit of a Billy Sims or a [Marcus] Dupree, he can persuade wallpaper to leave the wall.

Douglas S. Looney, sportswriter
Sports Illustrated, 1983

POP WARNER—Georgia, Cornell, Carlisle, Pittsburgh, Stanford, and Temple 1895–1935

What [Amos Alonzo] Stagg didn't invent, Pop Warner did.

John D. McCallum, sportswriter
Pac-Ten Football, 1982

PAUL WIGGIN—Stanford 1980–1983

Wiggin wears his personality on the top of his head. He has a flattop crewcut that looks as if a prankster glued a miniature aircraft carrier to his scalp.

Lowell Cohn, sports columnist
San Francisco Chronicle, 1982

FIELDING YOST—Ohio Wesleyan, Nebraska, Kansas, Stanford, and Michigan 1897–1941

Friend: Did you ever talk to Hurry Up Yost?
Lardner: No. My father taught me never to interrupt.

Ring Lardner, writer

COACHES: THE PROS

GEORGE ALLEN—Rams and Redskins 1966–1977

Halas: George Allen is a liar, a cheat, and a no-good S.O.B.
Lombardi: It looks to me like you've got yourself a winning coach.

Vince Lombardi, Packers coach, to
Bears owner George Halas when Dan
Reeves hired Allen to coach the Rams

His father gave him a six-week-old puppy when he was
four, and he traded it away for two twelve-year-old cats.

> Edward Bennett Williams, Redskins
> owner, on Allen's penchant for older
> players
> *Sports Illustrated,* 1971

Dierdorf: What happens if I look into the facemask of the
defensive end across from me—and I see an Eskimo?
Coryell: I wouldn't put it past George Allen, that cheatin'
sonofabitch.

> Don Coryell, Cardinals coach, to
> offensive lineman Dan Dierdorf

George seems incapable of having a good time—even in the
off-season. He doesn't do anything for fun but eat ice
cream.

> John McKay,
> Southern California coach
> *McKay: A Coach's Story,* 1975

It was more fun losing with other coaches than it was winning with George.

> Dan Reeves, former Rams owner
> *San Francisco Chronicle,* 1981

We gave him an unlimited expense account, and he's already exceeded it.

> Edward Bennett Williams,
> Redskins owner, a few weeks after
> he hired Allen
> New York *Daily News,* 1982

If George had his way, we'd probably be in a monastery
somewhere with the barbed wire and the gun turrets.

> Dave Butz, Redskins defensive tackle
> *San Francisco Examiner,* 1983

If George was a player's coach, I'd hate to see a coach's coach.

> John Matuszak, former defensive
> lineman
> *Cruisin' with the Tooz*, 1987

If you asked George Allen what time it was, he'd trade you a draft choice. If you asked him how his family was, he'd trade you a defensive back.

> Gene Klein, former Chargers owner
> *First Down and a Billion*, 1987

PAUL BROWN—BROWNS AND BENGALS 1946–1976

Paul Brown treated his players as if he had bought them at auction with a ring in their noses.

> Jim Murray, sports columnist
> *Los Angeles Times*

DON CORYELL—CARDINALS AND CHARGERS 1973–1986

I have seen guys look happier throwing up.

> Jim Murray
> *Los Angeles Times*

Here I am giving Dan Fouts a Most Valuable Player trophy in 1979 for being the first Chargers player to understand Coryell's offense.

> Gene Klein, Chargers owner,
> describing a photograph
> *First Down and a Billion*, 1987

MIKE DITKA—BEARS 1983–

Mike Ditka is a maniac. He could coach choir girls and make them bloodthirsty champions.

> Thomas "Hollywood" Henderson,
> former linebacker
> *Out of Control*, 1987

WEEB EWBANK—Colts and Jets 1954–1973

Weeb Ewbank can talk longer without saying anything than anyone I know.

Johnny Sample, former halfback and
defensive back
Confessions of a Dirty Ballplayer,
1970

TOM FLORES—Raiders 1979–1987

Flores's image is that he doesn't have an image. . . . Some coaches are headset-throwing maniacs on the sideline, some are cool . . . and then there's Flores, who looks like a guy waiting for a bus.

Scott Ostler, sports columnist
Los Angeles Times, 1983

ABE GIBRON—Bears 1972–1974

He was eating things we wouldn't even go swimming with in Alabama.

Charley Hannah, Buccaneers
offensive tackle, 1977

BUD GRANT—Vikings 1967–1985

In stark contrast to [Don] Shula, Viking coach Bud Grant spent most of Super Week acting like a Marine Corps drill sergeant with a terminal case of the piles.

Hunter S. Thompson, writer
Rolling Stone, 1974

If Tom Landry and Bud Grant had a personality contest, neither would win.

Don Meredith, former Cowboys
quarterback

The only place I ever looked forward to the prospect of interviewing Ol' Stoneface was in the loser's locker room at the Super Bowl.

John Lindblom, sportswriter
San Jose Mercury News,
1981

The longest dialogue I ever had with Bud was a monologue, and it lasted three words—"Get a haircut."

Joe Kapp, former Vikings quarterback
Sports Illustrated, 1985

GEORGE HALAS—BEARS 1920–1967

Halas: I signed Dick Butkus to a $200,000 contract.
Brickhouse: George, knowing you, that is $1,000 a year for 200 years.

Jack Brickhouse, Bears radio
broadcaster, to George Halas, 1965

He tosses nickels around like manhole covers.

Mike Ditka, former Bears tight end

I got along with Halas just fine. If he'd paid me a little more, I might have even liked him.

Doug Atkins, former Bears defensive
end
Sports Illustrated, 1982

Amazing. This is like Orville Wright coming back and deciding to run United Airlines.

Stan Jones, Broncos defensive line
coach, on Halas's return to help the
Bears at age eighty-seven
The Sporting News, 1982

Papa Halas is not really dead as long as one padded gladiator knocks the hell out of another for money and the sheer hell of it on a Saturday afternoon.

Ray Sons, sportswriter
Chicago Sun-Times, 1984

RED HICKEY—49ERS 1959–1963

Red didn't have much compassion for the players. He was in the service in World War II, and a sniper shot him in the heart. Red thought he missed.

Lon Simmons, 49ers broadcaster
San Jose Mercury News, 1979

CHUCK KNOX—RAMS, BILLS, AND SEAHAWKS 1973–

A press conference was called yesterday to announce the new head coach of the Rams. A limo pulled up, the passenger door was opened, and nobody got out.

Jim Murray, sports columnist
Los Angeles Times, 1973

Chuck Knox is a good offensive coach, but he doesn't know shit about defense.

Brian Bosworth, Seahawks linebacker
Village Voice, 1988

TOM LANDRY—COWBOYS 1960–1988

Eighty thousand people in the stands are going bananas, and there's Landry walking up and down trying to keep his hat on straight.

Don Rickles, comedian, 1966

Don't read Landry's playbook all the way through. Everybody dies at the end.

Peter Gent, former Cowboys receiver,
to a rookie
Newsweek, 1979

Landry would be up at the blackboard saying, "Okay, we'll
do this . . . then they'll do this . . . then we'll . . ." You'd interrupt him and say, "Coach, what if they *don't* do that?"
Landry would just look at you and say, "They will."

> Don Meredith, former Cowboys
> quarterback

He's a perfectionist. If he was married to Raquel Welch,
he'd expect her to cook.

> Don Meredith
> *Sports Illustrated*, 1979

Tendencies, man—that's what Landry's all about. . . . Landry does so much research that he knows what George
Allen is thinking at night while Allen is sitting alone in his
house.

> Thomas "Hollywood" Henderson,
> former Cowboys linebacker
> *Playboy*, 1981

I don't know. I only played there for nine years.

> Walt Garrison, former Cowboys
> running back, when asked if Landry
> ever smiles
> *San Francisco Chronicle*, 1981

This is something that probably doesn't happen in Tom
Landry's office.

> Sam Wyche, Bengals coach, after the
> team's pet cat vomited
> *Sports Illustrated*, 1984

VINCE LOMBARDI—PACKERS AND REDSKINS 1959–1970

I'm thirty-three years old, and I've got a family, and I've got
all the responsibilities in the world, and here I am hiding an
ice cream cone from the old man.

> Bob Skoronski, Packers offensive
> tackle, 1967

Lombardi has to have the highest threshold of pain in the world; none of our injuries hurts him at all.

> Jerry Kramer, Packers guard
> *Instant Replay*, 1968

He's fair. He treats us all the same—like dogs.

> Henry Jordan, Packers defensive
> lineman
> *The New York Times*, 1970

Nixon still speaks of Lombardi as if he might suddenly appear, at any moment, from underneath one of the larger rocks on the White House lawn.

> Hunter S. Thompson, writer
> "Fear and Loathing at the Super
> Bowl," 1974

When I heard this man was taking over the team in 1959, I could hardly wait to meet a man who went to church every day. I worked for him for two weeks, and then I realized this man *needs* to go to church every day.

> Bart Starr, former Packers
> quarterback, on Lombardi's profanity,
> 1976

In Green Bay we planned both babies for the off-season. Lombardi wouldn't have liked it during the season. We never thought about it—it was just the way it should be.

> Barbara Gregg, wife of former
> offensive lineman Forrest Gregg

The man named Lombardi was so competitive that he would drive ninety-five miles an hour just to reach a restaurant ahead of his friend [running back] Tony Canadeo and prove his route was better than Tony's.

> Red Smith, sportswriter
> *To Absent Friends from Red Smith*,
> 1982

You never know: God might think he's Vince Lombardi.

> Peter Gent, former Cowboys receiver
> and novelist
> *The Franchise,* 1983

He was so tough to work for that winning was the easy
way out.

> Willie Davis, former Packers
> defensive end
> *San Francisco Chronicle,* 1984

JOHNNY MAZUR—PATRIOTS 1970–1972

He went to Notre Dame, was an ex-Marine, and he smoked
cigars. Any one or even two of those things you can live
with, but not all three.

> Joe Kapp, former Patriots quarterback
> *Sports Illustrated,* 1982

JOHNNY "BLOOD" McNALLY—STEELERS 1937–1939

On most teams the coach worried about the players. With
Blood, the players worried about the coach.

> Art Rooney, Steelers owner, on the
> night-loving coach, 1975

CHUCK NOLL—STEELERS 1969–

Look at that face! I don't know what Chuck Noll had for
breakfast, but it wasn't quiche.

> Bob Costas, sportscaster
> "NFL Football," CBS-TV, 1981

BUM PHILLIPS—OILERS AND SAINTS 1975–1985

When he wears a single-breasted coat, as he did the other
day, he buttons all three buttons, which should tell you
something about his sartorial elegance.

> Jack Gallagher, sportswriter
> *Houston Post,* 1967

It reminds me of a good three-wood lie.

> Carol Mann, professional golfer, on
> Phillips' haircut
> *Sports Illustrated*, 1983

AL SAUNDERS—CHARGERS 1986–1988

Al Saunders sounds like a man delivering a eulogy for someone he has never met. This guy who is supposed to inspire the Chargers . . . could put a hungry newborn baby to sleep.

> T. J. Simers, sportswriter
> *San Diego Union*, 1988

HARLAND SVARE—RAMS AND CHARGERS 1962–1973

Harland Svare turned out to be the wrong man in the wrong job with the wrong team at the wrong time. Other than that, I'd made a fine selection.

> Gene Klein, former Chargers owner
> *First Down and a Billion*, 1987

ALLIE SHERMAN—GIANTS 1961–1968

Never trust a Jewish guy from Brooklyn who speaks with a Southern accent.

> Harold Rosenthal, sportswriter

DON SHULA—COLTS AND DOLPHINS 1963–

I'm fairly confident that if I died tomorrow, Don would find a way to preserve me until the season was over and he had time for a nice funeral.

> Dorothy Shula, wife of Don
> *Sports Illustrated*, 1981

I have never seen a statue that wouldn't look better with Shula's head on it.

> Pete Dexter, journalist
> *Esquire*, 1983

Shula down in Miami, he walks on water. But back in the old days, he missed a few stones along the way.

> Art Donovan, former Colts defensive
> tackle, on Shula's carousing
> "Late Night with David Letterman,"
> NBC-TV, 1983

He can take hisn and beat yourn, and he can take yourn and beat hisn.

> Bum Phillips, Saints coach
> *San Francisco Chronicle,* 1985

If a nuclear bomb is ever dropped on this country, the only things I'm certain will survive are AstroTurf and Don Shula.

> Bubba Paris, 49ers offensive tackle

BART STARR—PACKERS 1975–1983

When Vince Lombardi died, he must have taken Bart's brain with him.

> Dick Young, sports columnist
> *The Sporting News,* 1983

NORM VAN BROCKLIN—VIKINGS AND FALCONS 1961–1974

A guy with the nice, even disposition of a top sergeant whose shoes are too tight.

> Jim Murray, sports columnist
> *Los Angeles Times,* 1986

BILL WALSH—49ERS 1979–1988

You half expect his headset is playing Mozart.

> Jim Murray
> *Los Angeles Times,* 1982

Bill Walsh's system could make me a good quarterback, and I can't throw the ball in the ocean from the beach.

> Jerry Glanville, Falcons defensive
> coordinator
> *Inside Sports,* 1982

In 1981 the Giants scouted him before their play-off game. They studied three games and threw up their hands. He'd called fifty-two different plays on first-and-ten.

> Paul Zimmerman, football analyst
> *The New Thinking Man's Guide to*
> *Pro Football,* 1984

 **COLLEGE FOOTBALL**

No athletic director holds office longer than two losing football coaches.

> Bob Zuppke, Illinois coach

I do not see the relationship of these highly industrialized affairs on Saturday afternoons to higher learning in America.

> Robert Maynard Hutchins, University
> of Chicago president

A sport that bears the same relation to education that bullfighting does to agriculture.

> Elbert Hubbard, writer, on college
> football

If it meant the betterment of Michigan State, our football team would play any eleven gorillas from Barnum & Bailey any Saturday.

> John A. Hannah, Michigan State
> president

If lessons are learned in defeat, as they say, our team is really getting a great education.

> Murray Warmath, Northwestern
> coach
> *Sports Illustrated*, 1958

Football is a box connected by a thread to the university. The box is opened on Saturday, the players come out, perform, then go back in the box. They aren't really students.

> James Van Allen, University of Iowa
> professor, 1959

Our game plan is first year, a .500 season. Second year, a conference championship. Third year, undefeated. Fourth, a national championship. And by the fifth year, we'll be on probation, of course.

> Bear Bryant, Alabama coach,
> 1958

Question: Two teams that have lost thirteen games between them, couldn't hold Manual Arts scoreless, and ran up seven points between them last week while their opposition was scoring eighty-three, met in the season's finale. What do we call it?
Answer: The Big Game.

> Jim Murray, sports columnist, on
> California–Stanford game,
> 1961

I don't expect to win enough games to be put on NCAA probation. I just want to win enough to warrant an investigation.

> Bob Devaney, Nebraska coach,
> 1962

A school without football is in danger of deteriorating into a medieval study hall.

> Vince Lombardi, Packers coach

The colleges would do better to get rid of the night games and return to Saturday afternoon football the way God and Grantland Rice created it.

> John Hall, sportswriter

My players can wear their hair as long as they want and dress any way they want. That is, if they can pay their own tuition.

> Eddie Robinson, Grambling State
> coach
> *Sports Illustrated,* 1971

Football is not a democracy. There's nothing to debate. The players can debate in political science class.

> Carl De Pasqua, University of
> Pittsburgh coach

It's kind of hard to rally around a math class.

> Bear Bryant, Alabama coach
> *Sports Illustrated,* 1973

Just remember one thing. I can do *your* job, but you can't do *mine!*

> Woody Hayes, Ohio State coach, to a
> professor who criticized football

Although the NCAA frowns upon it, many football players are provided with brand-new cars; the rest of the student body is prohibited from roller skating on campus.

> Larry Linderman, journalist
> *Penthouse,* 1982

If you look at his grades, you'll realize he doesn't know the meaning of many words.

> Bobby Bowden, Florida State coach,
> who said linebacker Reggie Herring
> didn't know the meaning of the word
> "fear," 1982

I want a guy who, when he crosses the white lines, is the toughest, meanest, most aggressive guy. Then, after the game, he takes a shower, puts on a three-piece suit, opens the door for ladies, uses correct English, and has manners when he eats.

> George Perles, Michigan State coach
> *The Sporting News,* 1983

Why not hire football players like groundskeepers are hired? I know many people on this campus who like demolition derbies, but the university is no place for a demolition derby.

> Julian Smith, University of Florida
> professor
> *The Sporting News,* 1983

If you go to college and don't get an education, you come out four years later unable to do anything. The janitor has been on campus seventeen years, and how much has it helped him?

> Harry Edwards, University of
> California sociologist
> *The Sporting News,* 1983

It gets down to the W's and L's. Nobody talks about grades or moral victories. As someone said, we don't line up at the fifty to exchange transcripts.

> Paul Wiggin, Stanford coach
> *The Sporting News,* 1983

College football takes a bunch of kids off the street and exposes them to something besides car theft and armed robbery.

> Dan Jenkins, sportswriter and
> novelist
> *Life Its Ownself,* 1984

My question is, after arriving early in August to three-a-day practices in one-hundred-degree heat, and then moving into an eleven-week season that takes a minimum of sixty hours a week in meetings, practice, and travel, and then into a conditioning program until spring practice starts, who's the guy that called a football scholarship "a free ride"?

> Quintin Schonewise, Kansas
> offensive tackle
> *Sports Illustrated,* 1984

This is the first and probably last time you'll sit on the fifty-yard line.

> Harold Shapiro, University of
> Michigan president, to graduating
> seniors
> *Sports Illustrated,* 1984

Everybody thinks Bill is going to get an engineering degree at Pitt, but his major is really golf and sex.

> Bill Fralic, Sr., on Bill, Jr., an
> offensive lineman
> *The Sporting News,* 1985

A good football program is one where the students take the administration building demanding more tickets.

> Lou Holtz, University of Minnesota
> coach
> *USA Today,* 1985

I thought I did until I looked at some old game films.

> Bum Phillips, Saints coach, when
> asked if he played college ball
> *The Sporting News,* 1986

Some college and high school teams run out on the field
and jump up and down, pound each other, and that's more
contact than they have in the game.

> John Madden, CBS-TV broadcaster
> *One Knee Equals Two Feet,* 1986

The NCAA is into "amateurism." The schools are into academics. . . . [But] what they are really into is money.

> Lawrence Taylor, Giants linebacker
> *LT: Living on the Edge,* 1987

We bent the rules, but not like now. I was watching the
game between Florida State and Miami. They should've
started it with a burglar alarm.

> Darrell Royal, former Texas coach
> *Sports Illustrated,* 1987

What a story! Sex, blackmail, payoffs. I thought I was reading about college football in Texas.

> Johnny Carson, on the "holy war"
> among television preachers
> "The Tonight Show," NBC-TV, 1988

If you're a football star in Oklahoma, you're right up there
with the pope and a thousand-dollar-a-night hooker; everybody wants a piece of you.

> Thomas "Hollywood" Henderson,
> former linebacker
> *Out of Control,* 1988

I didn't realize how important the Heisman Trophy was
until everybody who came over to the house said, "Where's
the trophy?"

> Marcus Allen, Raiders running back
> "NFL Football," NBC-TV, 1989

COLLEGES AND UNIVERSITIES

ALABAMA *CRIMSON TIDE*

Hell, at Alabama my junior year, when we lost two games, the word was: Rebuild.

> Joe Namath, Jets quarterback
> *I Can't Wait Until Tomorrow . . . ,*
> 1969

When we have a good team at Alabama, I know it's because we have boys who come from good mamas and papas.

> Bear Bryant, Alabama coach

In Alabama, Coach Bryant is second only to God. We believe that on the eighth day the Lord created the Crimson Tide.

> Jeremiah Denton, U.S. senator from
> Alabama
> *Sports Illustrated,* 1982

ARKANSAS *RAZORBACKS*

Our players don't do dances in the end zone. We like them to act like they've been there before.

> Lou Holtz, Arkansas coach
> *Life,* 1984

BRIGHAM YOUNG *COUGARS*

No one outside of the Osmond family thinks that BYU was the best team in the country in 1984.

> Allen Barra, sportswriter
> *Inside Sports,* 1985

How can you rank BYU number one? Who'd they play, Bo Diddley Tech?

> Bryant Gumbel, broadcaster
> "Today," NBC-TV, 1985

I think they expected us all to have three wives, all with dresses that never came above the ankle.

Glen Kozlowski, BYU receiver, when
the team played Boston College at the
Meadowlands in New Jersey
Sports Illustrated, 1985

CALIFORNIA *GOLDEN BEARS*

I don't mind getting run over by a tank, but we got run over this week by a moped.

Jim Walden, Washington State
coach, after losing to Cal 31–21
The Sporting News, 1986

CALIFORNIA STATE FULLERTON *TITANS*

They called us Cal-State Disneyland, and we took them right to the Haunted House.

Ron McLean, Fullerton defensive
tackle, after beating Hawaii, 1986

CALIFORNIA STATE HAYWARD *PIONEERS*

We tried to think up something native to Hayward, but all we could think of was zucchinis.

Dennis Lavery, Hayward State public
relations director, looking for a new
nickname
Seattle Post-Intelligencer, 1984

CLEMSON *TIGERS*

Hell, folks used to ask if a Clemson was a fruit or a vegetable.

Frank Howard, Clemson coach
Sports Illustrated, 1982

COLUMBIA *TIGERS*

One of sports' most treasured records—Columbia's losing streak—stood in grave danger at halftime Saturday, with the starving Lions stomping Villanova 28–14. Fortunately . . . Columbia rallied to beat itself 34–42 and ran its string of consecutive drubbings to twenty-eight.

> Steve Harvey, syndicated columnist,
> 1986

I don't feel like I choked. It was either the wind or the full moon or the tides or gravity or something.

> Kurt Dasbach, after he missed a field
> goal against Dartmouth that would
> have ended Columbia's 38-game
> losing streak, 1987

To liberals, to beat somebody on the field is morally aggressive. . . . If we ever won the Ivy League title, the administration would have us investigated by the American Civil Liberties Union.

> D. Keith Mano, writer and Columbia
> graduate
> *Sports Illustrated,* 1986

DUKE *BLUE DEVILS*

If you asked the alumni if they'd rather have a Nobel prize-winning graduate or a Heisman Trophy winner, 95 percent would take the Heisman.

> Beano Cook, football analyst
> *Sport,* 1983

If it didn't have classes, Duke would have made a great country club.

> Ben Bennett, Duke quarterback
> *Sport,* 1983

HOFSTRA *FLYING DUTCHMEN*

A billion people in China don't know we play. What's worse, a lot of people in our own area don't know it, either.

> Mickey Kwiatkowski, Hofstra coach
> *Sports Illustrated*, 1981

ILLINOIS *FIGHTING ILLINI*

There are three big sports at Illinois: football, basketball, and fund-raising.

> Neale Stoner, Illinois athletic director
> *Chicago Tribune*, 1986

KANSAS *JAYHAWKS*

Who's the one guy who thinks we can do it?

> Mike Gottfried, Kansas coach, when
> told his odds against winning the Big
> Eight were one hundred to one
> *Sports Illustrated*, 1984

The bigger the game, the better Danny Bradley plays. Give him the eyes of Texas, and he'll gouge 'em. Give him the Cornhuskers of Nebraska, and he'll shuck 'em. Give him the Jayhawks of Kansas, and he's liable to darned near fall asleep.

> Danny Bradley, Oklahoma
> quarterback
> *The Daily Oklahoman*, 1984

KANSAS STATE *WILDCATS*

Kansas State hasn't won a Big Eight championship in forty years. I told them if I don't win a championship in the same length of time, I'll resign.

> Jim Dickey, Kansas State coach
> *Sports Illustrated*, 1979

I hate to think it has been ninety-three years of bad luck.

> Bill Miller, Kansas State athletic
> director, on the team's 299–509–41
> record, worst in Division I-A, 1989

MARYLAND *TERRAPINS*

The University of Maryland football team members all make straight A's. Their B's are a little crooked.

> Johnny Walker, Baltimore disc jockey
> *Sports Illustrated*, 1978

The crowd sang "Maryland, My Maryland" after each touchdown, even the four they called back. By the end of the first quarter I knew all the words.

> Jack Rothrock, who in 1945 played
> for Guilford College in a 60–6 loss to
> Maryland
> *Sports Illustrated*, 1981

MIAMI *HURRICANES*

It's unfair that anyone should have a chance for a good tan and the mythical national championship.

> Joe Gergen, sports columnist
> *The Sporting News*, 1986

The Hurricanes look weak in the departments in which they dominated college football in 1986: dormitory riots, illegally leased cars, shoplifting, and telephone misuse.

> Steve Harvey, syndicated columnist,
> 1987

Jerome Brown contributed mightily to the mounting penalty toll. A former Miami Hurricane, he probably majored in penalties.

> Pete Axthelm, sportscaster, on the
> Eagles defensive tackle
> "NFL PrimeTime," ESPN-TV, 1989

MICHIGAN STATE *SPARTANS*

It isn't so much what their first and second teams do to you—but the third, fourth, and fifth teams simply murder you!

> Ray George, Texas A&M coach, after
> losing 48–6 to the Spartans, 1951

MICHIGAN *WOLVERINES*

The team still is despondent over the finding of the state sesquicentennial commission that the wolverine never inhabited Michigan. Or Pasadena, California.

> Steve Harvey, syndicated columnist,
> 1987

MINNESOTA *GOPHERS*

We don't have summer, just a season in the middle of the year when the sledding is poor.

> Bronko Nagurski, former Minnesota
> tackle

We will get the heart and soul of our football team from the state of Minnesota. However, we'll have to go elsewhere for the arms and legs.

> Lou Holtz, University of Minnesota
> coach
> *Chicago Sun-Times,* 1985

Everybody up here has blond hair and a blue nose.

> Lou Holtz
> *The Sporting News,* 1985

MONTANA STATE *BOBCATS*

We definitely will be improved this year. Last year we lost ten games. This year we only scheduled nine.

> Ray Jenkins, Montana State coach
> *Sports Illustrated,* 1959

NEBRASKA *CORNHUSKERS*

We finally got Nebraska where we want them—off the schedule.

Cal Stolle, University of Minnesota
coach

Watching Nebraska break the huddle is like watching six refrigerators roll down a hill.

Rex Norris, Oklahoma defensive line
coach
The Sporting News, 1982

Ten fullbacks? Seven nose guards? That's not a depth chart. That's the free world.

Terry Donahue, UCLA coach, on
Nebraska's spring roster
Sports Illustrated, 1983

They had twenty-four players who are married. We don't have twenty-four players old enough to date.

Jerry Stovall, Louisiana State coach
The Sporting News, 1983

I've never seen anyone kick off so much.

Mike Gottfried, Kansas coach
Sports Illustrated, 1983

You know that big "N" on the side of the football stadium— the first thing you see when you come into town from the airport? Well, a lot of people think we're just a football school, but we also emphasize academics. That "N" really stands for "knowledge."

Bill Harris, mayor of Lincoln,
Nebraska, 1987

NORTH CAROLINA *TAR HEELS*

Yep, right on schedule: The leaves have started to fall, and so has North Carolina's football team.

Jack McCallum, sportswriter
Sports Illustrated, 1983

NORTHWESTERN *WILDCATS*

We gave up a long time ago on trying to get the crowds cheering for touchdowns and field goals. Instead, we now try to get them excited when the Wildcats actually catch a punt.

Steve DePalma, Northwestern
cheerleader, on the 0–11 team that
was outscored 505–82, 1981

We're not on the bottom of the world. We're beneath it.

Tim Salem, Northwestern
quarterback, after their thirty-fourth
straight loss
Sports Illustrated, 1982

NOTRE DAME *FIGHTING IRISH*

Outlined against a blue-gray October sky, the Four Horse-men rode again. In dramatic lore they are known as Fam-ine, Pestilence, Destruction, and Death. These are only aliases. Their real names are Stuhldreher, Miller, Crowley, and Layden. They formed the crest of the South Bend cy-clone before which another fighting Army football team was swept over the precipice at the Polo Grounds yesterday afternoon as fifty-five thousand spectators peered down on the bewildering panorama spread on the green plain below.

Grantland Rice, lead paragraph,
Notre Dame–Army
New York Herald-Tribune, 1924

If no one else had, Notre Dame would surely have invented football later on.

Dan Jenkins, sportswriter
Saturday's America, 1970

Every priest and nun in the country is a potential recruiter. When I was an eighth grader at St. Mary's in Poughkeepsie,

New York, the nun used to line us up to say a prayer for
Notre Dame.

> Monty Stickles, former Notre Dame
> tight end
> *San Francisco Chronicle,* 1984

I love my wife dearly and have been married for twenty-five
years. But if Linda Evans calls . . .

> Lou Holtz, University of Minnesota
> coach, leaving his option open for
> Notre Dame
> *The Sporting News,* 1986

I certainly wasn't smart enough to get in academically. . . . I
guess the standards for being a coach are lower.

> Lou Holtz, on taking the Notre Dame
> job
> *The Fighting Spirit,* 1989

There are two kinds of people in the world, Notre Dame lov-
ers and Notre Dame haters. And, quite frankly, they're both
a pain in the ass.

> Dan Devine, former Notre Dame
> coach
> *San Francisco Chronicle,* 1988

OHIO STATE *BUCKEYES*

Every week Ohio State would fill up with over eighty-
thousand spectators, and every week the highlight of the
game would be that daring moment when Woody tried a lat-
eral.

> Dan Jenkins, sportswriter, on coach
> Woody Hayes
> *Sports Illustrated,* 1968

This is the first time I've met Woody Hayes, and I've never
been in Columbus, but I don't like either of them.

> Darryl Rogers, Michigan State coach,
> 1976

The network may not show the game. There's already too much violence on TV.

> Lou Holtz, University of Minnesota
> coach, having misgivings about
> playing Ohio State
> *The Sporting News*, 1985

OKLAHOMA *SOONERS*

Other people and teams across the country dream about winning. We invented it.

> Barry Switzer, Oklahoma coach
> *The Sporting News*, 1986

Vinny Testaverde did more harm to Oklahoma in three-and-a-half hours than John Steinbeck did in three hundred pages.

> Joe Gergen, sports columnist, after
> Miami beat Oklahoma 28–16
> *The Sporting News*, 1986

OREGON *DUCKS*

The Oregon Ducks during my years were some football team, a cross between the Bad News Bears, the Wild Bunch, the Miami Dolphins, and the Rolling Stones.

> Ahmad Rashad, former receiver, on
> the late 1960s
> *Rashad*, 1988

OREGON STATE *BEAVERS*

Bear Bryant's widow has moved to Corvallis. She wanted to get as far away from football as she could.

> Glenn Dickey, sports columnist
> *San Francisco Chronicle*, 1983

Would you rather rebuild at Oklahoma or have everyone back at Oregon State?

> Beano Cook, football analyst
> *The Oregonian*, 1988

PENN STATE *NITTANY LIONS*

You can't be too rich, too thin, or have too many Penn State linebackers.

Marv Levy, Bills coach
Sports Illustrated, 1987

PENNSYLVANIA *QUAKERS*

Cut the pep talks. There's been too much talking at this university and not enough playing.

Mike Christiani, Pennsylvania
linebacker, 1985

PURDUE *BOILERMAKERS*

Purdue University is the Big Ten's contribution to ethnic jokes. . . . To have any class you've got to come from a cooled-out school like Wisconsin or Michigan or Northwestern. Purdue? Man, Purdue is like Iowa.

Dan Jenkins, sportswriter
Saturday's America, 1970

RICE *OWLS*

We don't have a sheltered curriculum for the athletes in this school. They can't take courses like marble shooting, underwater kissing, trees and shrubs.

Ray Alborn, Rice coach

The typical Rice student would be someone you talk to at eye level, but when he talks back, he's talking over your head.

Tommy Kramer, former Rice
quarterback
Inside Sports, 1983

SOUTHERN CALIFORNIA *TROJANS*

I understand the TV show "That's Incredible!" has been filming on the USC campus. They shot twelve football players attending class at the same time.

> George Raveling, Washington State
> basketball coach
> *Sports Illustrated*, 1980

I love to watch the USC football players stand in line because it looks like evolution.

> Byron Allen, comedian
> "Evening at the Improv," NBC-TV,
> 1982

I had geography class at night, and all the football players would attend it. You could tell who they were: They were the guys in the back with the girls on their laps yelling and screaming.

> Bill Lee, former major-league pitcher
> and USC graduate
> *The Wrong Stuff*, 1984

We'd like our receivers to have both speed and quickness. But if they had both, they'd be at USC.

> LaVell Edwards, Brigham Young
> coach
> *Chicago Tribune*, 1986

The game was played in the land of "Let's do lunch."

> Bob Ley, sportscaster
> "Sportscenter," ESPN-TV, 1989

SOUTHERN METHODIST *MUSTANGS*

I've been wearin' Levi's and T-shirts all my life. I think I want to go someplace where they wear those pants with no belts and those loafers with those funny little tassels on 'em.

> Don Meredith, quarterback,
> preferring SMU over Texas Christian

All good J. R. Ewings send their Lucys to SMU, where they can major in cheerleading. The mascot ought to be the Izod alligator.

Skip Bayless, sportswriter
Sport, 1982

I don't have a job. They don't have a team. We'd both have to be interested.

Earle Bruce, former Ohio State
coach, considering SMU
Sports Illustrated, 1987

STANFORD *CARDINAL*

I've never been able to understand all those words they use at Stanford.

Joe Kapp, California coach
San Jose Mercury News, 1982

It even rains soft out here.

Paul Hornung, sportscaster
"College Football," WTBS-TV, 1985

TEXAS CHRISTIAN *HORNED FROGS*

The TCU Horned Frogs stayed in the thick of the football game right up, and almost all the way through, the opening kickoff.

Dan Jenkins, sportswriter and
novelist
Baja, California, 1981

TEXAS *LONGHORNS*

For generations after its founding in 1881, the University of Texas at Austin seemed to have only one long-range game plan: its football program.

Time, 1982

They remind me of a piranha around a chunk of meat.
They're always making that water splash.

> Grant Teaff, Baylor coach, on the
> Texas defenders
> *Sports Illustrated,* 1983

TEXAS TECH *RED RAIDERS*

We're working on throwing in the spring. We'll work on
catching in the fall.

> David McWilliams, Texas Tech coach
> *Sports Illustrated,* 1986

TULANE *GREEN WAVE*

I don't think we ought to execute them right now. Give
them another two or three weeks and see if they improve.

> Mack Brown, Tulane coach, when
> asked about his team's execution
> *The Sporting News,* 1986

Coaching defense at Tulane for the past two years has been
sort of like being the rear guy in a horse costume. The view
hasn't been too good.

> Bill Shaw, Tulane defensive
> coordinator, 1987

UCLA *BRUINS*

Most of us are out of public high schools like everyone else.
We're the same kind of football players who go to UCLA,
except we can read.

> Mike Wyman, Stanford defensive
> lineman
> *Seattle Post-Intelligencer,* 1984

Man, at least we don't wear *pastels.* That's their color, isn't
it? *Pastel* blue and gold? Man, I hate it. They don't come

right at you . . . they try to finesse you, pansy you. Man, they play *girls'* football.

Brian Bosworth, Oklahoma linebacker
Sports Illustrated, 1986

VANDERBILT *COMMODORES*

Playing Vanderbilt is like having an off-week.

Steve Kiner, Tennessee linebacker,
1969

My special trouble is that I am now head-coaching one of the teams I'd want to play.

Steve Sloan, Vanderbilt coach
Sports Illustrated, 1973

Inflation killed the Vanderbilt Commodores Saturday. Once the football was inflated, Vanderbilt was dead.

Jimmy Bryan, sportswriter, on a 66–3
loss to Alabama
Birmingham News, 1979

WAKE FOREST *DEMON DEACONS*

Our biggest mistake was not taking Wake Forest lightly enough.

Larry Lacewell, Oklahoma assistant
coach, after beating Wake Forest
63–0, 1974

WASHINGTON *HUSKIES*

I admire them, I respect them, but I hate them.

Jim Walden, Washington State coach
Sports Illustrated, 1986

WASHINGTON STATE *COUGARS*

Washington State is without question one of the best teams in the nation at coming from behind. Unfortunately, Washington State is also one of the best teams at getting behind.

Jim Walden, Washington State coach
Seattle Post-Intelligencer, 1985

WILLIAM AND MARY *INDIANS*

We had too many Marys and not enough Williams.

> Lou Holtz, William and Mary coach,
> when he lost 26–18 to Cincinnati,
> 1969

WISCONSIN *BADGERS*

Wisconsin has a Lawrence Welk offense—a one, a two, a three, and a punt.

> Mel Proctor, sportscaster
> "College Football," WTBS-TV, 1986

YALE *ELIS*

All football comes from Yale.

> Knute Rockne, Notre Dame coach

At some universities, athletes are treated like kings; snap your fingers and it's yours. Try snapping your fingers for a glass of water at Yale, and you could die of thirst.

> Jeff Rohrer, former Yale linebacker
> *The New York Times*, 1986

 **DEFENSIVE BACKS**

The receivers throw head fakes at you. They throw body fakes. I can follow two fakes, but when they throw three at you . . . well, it means somebody isn't getting to the quarterback.

> Dick "Night Train" Lane, Lions
> cornerback

The toughest thing for me was to pick up a loose receiver. My job was all angles. On a blackboard you always made the angles intersect, but out there the chalk didn't always get there on time.

Bill Baird, Jets safety

All through college I was one of the glory guys, quarterback, wide receiver, and shit, here I am on defense.

Charlie Waters, Cowboys defensive
back, 1970

I don't think you can describe it, the anguish and challenge of playing it. It's like walking on eggs.

Mel Blount, Steelers cornerback

If a defensive back allows himself to become honed in on, he will be unemployed in the near future.

Lester Hayes, Raiders cornerback

I was on the football team for a week. They put me at safety. . . . It was not easy for a 103-pound safety to stop a 200-pound running back. Toward the end of the practice, when the coach told me to get back in there, I asked him if he'd mind painting me white so that I could disguise myself as a yard marker.

Robin Williams, actor/comedian
Playboy, 1982

Tony Retting is the kind of kid you like to have in there because he foams at the mouth and chases cars.

Bill McCartney, Colorado coach, on
his defensive back
The Sporting News, 1982

The whole team even took ballet lessons last spring. I just know I'll be going up to knock down a pass and hear "Swan Lake" in the back of my mind.

Mark Robinson, Penn State safety
Sports Illustrated, 1983

Cornerbacks have the toughest job on the field. I don't envy them for a minute. I don't miss being over there. I like being able to sleep the night before a game.

> Roy Green, Cardinals cornerback-
> turned-receiver
> *USA Today,* 1984

It's a lonely man's position, and if I had it to do over, I'd get me a set of golf clubs.

> Lester Hayes, Raiders cornerback
> *San Francisco Chronicle,* 1984

MIKE BATTLE—JETS 1969–1970

Battle was the guy who played on the Jets, hung out with Namath, and ate shot glasses to help get up for a game.

> Bill Lee
> *The Wrong Stuff,* 1984

RON BOLTON—PATRIOTS AND BROWNS 1972–1982

He's in a class by himself, or should I say a lack of class all by himself.

> Lynn Swann, Steelers receiver, after
> he claimed Bolton spit in his face, 1981

LESTER HAYES—RAIDERS 1977–1986

Hayes has psyched himself to the point where he really thinks he's the one going out for the pass. In practice, when that happens, I wind up as the cornerback. That's not the way it's supposed to be.

> Cliff Branch, Raiders receiver
> *San Jose Mercury News,* 1981

DON ROGERS—BROWNS 1984–1985

He'll cause a lot of receivers to hear a cat sipping milk at one hundred yards.

> Sam Rutigliano, Browns coach
> *Sports Illustrated,* 1984

ANTHONY WASHINGTON—Redskins and Steelers 1981–1984

Anthony Washington . . . zigs when he should zag and ends up watching many pass completions from the seat of his pants.

Lowell Cohn, sportswriter
San Francisco Chronicle, 1984

CHARLIE WATERS—Cowboys 1970–1981

A rolling ball of butcher knives.

Blackie Sherrod, sportswriter
Dallas Times-Herald

DONNELL WOOLFORD—Bears 1989–

No matter where the ball is, if he's around it, it seems to end up in the other guy's hands.

Joe Theismann, sportscaster
"NFL PrimeTime," ESPN-TV, 1989

 **DEFENSIVE LINEMEN**

I tackle everybody and then throw them away until I come to the one with the ball.

Gene "Big Daddy" Lipscomb, Colts
defensive tackle

Quarterbacks and tight ends die comfortably, in big beds, and the Irish setter is whimpering on the other side of the door, and someone is mowing the great lawn outside the big mansion. But the linemen give it up in these little rooms in the poor sections.

Alex Karras, former Lions defensive
tackle

It helps if you don't have a brain. If you took all the nose guards in the league and put them on the field, half of them would probably be drunk and the others merely lunatics.

> Jerry Boyarsky, Saints nose tackle
> *The Sporting News*, 1981

Sacks are garbage stats. One guy does all the work, and the other one gets the sack.

> Joe Galat, former Oilers coach
> *Sports Illustrated*, 1982

Oh, sacks? I thought you said sex. Sacks are the second-best thing.

> Tom Keating, former Raiders
> defensive tackle
> *Sports Illustrated*, 1982

If me and King Kong went into an alley, only one of us would come out. And it wouldn't be the monkey.

> Lyle Alzado, Raiders defensive end
> *Sport*, 1983

Being a nose tackle is like being the fire hydrant at a dog show.

> Doug Dieken, Browns offensive
> tackle
> *Seattle Post-Intelligencer*, 1984

LYLE ALZADO—BRONCOS, BROWNS, AND RAIDERS 1971–1984

There was something else about him that helped him make it in football. He had a nasty streak.

> Jack Martilotta, childhood friend

Putting a Rutgers man alongside Lyle Alzado would seem to smack of putting a nun in the Mafia.

> Jim Murray, sports columnist, on
> nose guard Bill Pickel
> *Los Angeles Times*, 1986

DOUG ATKINS—Bears 1955–1967

Playing opposite Doug Atkins is like having your pants
taken down in front of sixty thousand people.

John Gonzaga, Lions offensive tackle,
1963

COY BACON—Rams, Chargers, Bengals, and Redskins 1968–1981

He is a fern brain—if he had any less of an IQ, he would be
a plant in a botany class.

Stan Walters, Eagles offensive tackle
San Jose Mercury News, 1980

ELVIN BETHEA—Oilers 1968–1983

He doesn't get hurt. He's a hurter, not a hurtee.

Bum Phillips, Oilers coach
"Thursday Night Edition," ABC-TV,
1980

LES BINGAMAN—Lions 1948–1954

One day, during a practice break, one of his teammates
yelled, "Move around, Bing, you're killing the grass."

Alex Karras, former Lions defensive
tackle
Even Big Guys Cry, 1977

DAN BIRDWELL—Raiders 1962–1964

I've got bruises all over my body from bumping into Dan
around the kitchen. Or taking a gouge from him while he's
asleep. He won't even play with our three children for fear
of injuring them.

Diane Birdwell, wife of Dan

JERRY BOYARSKY—SAINTS, BENGALS, AND PACKERS 1981–

Jerry's the kind of kid you'd like anywhere on your team. . . . Well, maybe you wouldn't want him at cornerback.

Bum Phillips, Saints coach

FRED DEAN—CHARGERS AND 49ERS 1975–1985

You could try to block Dean with a pickup truck, and it wouldn't work. He's too good, too fast, and no rules committee is ever going to stop him.

Pat Haden, Rams quarterback
Sports Illustrated, 1982

Cars and women gave Fred more trouble than opposing linemen.

Gene Klein, former Chargers owner
First Down and a Billion, 1987

MARK GASTINEAU—JETS 1981–

Against Green Bay he did [a sack dance] after one of mine. I told him, "If you're going to dance, do it on your own sacks."

Marty Lyons, Jets defensive tackle
Sports Illustrated, 1982

He's like Felix Unger, a total neat freak. He keeps his cereal boxes in alphabetical order.

Lisa Gastineau, wife of Mark
Inside Sports, 1985

"MEAN JOE" GREENE—STEELERS 1969–1981

Help him up after a play, pat him on the backside, talk to him. Keep him happy. If you get him angry, he's liable to hurt somebody.

Bud Grant, Vikings coach, 1973

CLAUDE HUMPHREY—FALCONS AND STEELERS 1968–1981

Certain days of the week the children and I stay in our place. We steer clear of him on Fridays.

> Sandra Humphrey, wife of Claude
> *San Francisco Examiner,* 1981

ED "TOO TALL" JONES—COWBOYS 1974–1989

If the head slap were still legal in the NFL, Ed Jones would go down as the greatest defensive end of all time.

> Ernie Stautner, Cowboys defensive
> coordinator
> *San Francisco Examiner,* 1983

LOUIE KELCHER—CHARGERS AND 49ERS 1975– 1984

George, if you can block the Coke machine, you can block Kelcher.

> John Madden, Raiders coach to guard
> George Buehler

Even our scouts had him timed in the forty-yard dash as slightly slower than a cloud on a windless day.

> Gene Klein, former Chargers owner
> *First Down and a Billion,* 1987

JOE KLECKO—JETS AND COLTS 1977–1988

He does some things you just can't copy, like grabbing his opponent by the shoulders and just walking him back to the quarterback.

> Doug Martin, Vikings defensive
> tackle
> *Sports Illustrated,* 1982

GENE "BIG DADDY" LIPSCOMB—Rams, Colts, and Steelers 1953–1962

He probably woke up in a bad mood this morning because the dirt is flying in his vicinity and our guards are coming out of it like drunks being tossed from a saloon.

Alex Karras, Lions defensive tackle,
1962

JOHN "THE TOOZ" MATUSZAK—Oilers, Chiefs, and Raiders 1973–1982

He sports a mug that resembles the sort of hood ornament Screamin' Jay Hawkins might have mounted on his '55 DeSoto to ward off unfriendly spirits.

Mark Jacobson, writer
Esquire, 1985

He was a giant among giants! Even crazy guys thought he was nuts!

Glen Waggoner, sportswriter
Esquire, 1988

MERLIN OLSEN—Rams 1962–1976

Merlin Olsen is very big, very strong, has great speed and great agility, is a very smart ballplayer, gives at least 110 percent on every play, and those are his weak points.

Jerry Kramer, Packers guard
Instant Replay, 1968

Merlin Olsen went swimming in Loch Ness—and the monster got out.

Jim Murray, sports columnist

WILLIAM "THE REFRIGERATOR" PERRY—Bears 1985–

William is just a biscuit away from three-fifty.

Dan Hampton, Bears defensive end,
1985

The best use of fat since the invention of bacon.

Mike Royko, columnist
Chicago Sun-Times, 1985

When he goes into a restaurant, he doesn't ask for a menu, he asks for an estimate.

Tony Kornheiser, sportswriter
The Washington Post, 1986

MIKE REID—Bengals 1970–1974

I've had games against him when I swear I never touched him once.

Dave Herman, Jets guard

LEE ROY SELMON—Buccaneers 1976–1985

At halftime I told the coach my deepest secrets. I said I never wanted to be buried at sea, I never wanted to get hit in the mouth with a hockey puck, and I didn't want to go out and play that second half against Lee Roy Selmon.

Ted Albrecht, Bears offensive tackle

RANDY WHITE—Cowboys 1975–1988

The guard came up to me and said, "I can't block him." Just like that, "I can't block him." You don't know how frightening that was. I looked at the guy and wanted to say, "What do you want me to do? Do you want to throw the ball and have *me* try to block him?"

Pat Haden, Rams quarterback
Sports Illustrated, 1982

 DIET AND EXERCISE

If a man is in decent condition and takes the proper training, the game is not dangerous in any special sense. There are worse things in college life than a sprained ankle, a twisted knee, or a broken nose.

> Walter Camp, Yale coach, 1893

I needed to lose a few pounds, but that was a tough way to do it.

> Earl Morrall, Lions quarterback, after clipping off his big toe with a lawnmower, 1963

When I was weighed, I used to put two five-pound weights in the waistband of my jock. The needle hit 240, and Jim Myers, the Cowboys line coach, would say, "You don't look that heavy. I guess you've just got a real solid build."

> Mike Connelly, Cowboys center

I've never seen a mean fat guy.

> Vince Lombardi, Packers coach

I kick with my foot, not with my arms.

> Toni Fritsch, Cowboys placekicker, refusing to lift weights, 1971

Jogging is my idea of nothing to do.

> Merlin Olsen, former Rams defensive tackle
> *Sports Illustrated,* 1981

I didn't weigh him. I'm not planning on auctioning him off.

Bum Phillips, Saints coach, on
quarterback Ken Stabler
San Francisco Chronicle, 1982

The coaches thought he would be All-Pro. He turned out to be All-Cafeteria.

Ladd Herzog, Oilers general
manager, on 330-pound lineman
Angelo Fields, a number-two draft
pick and a bust
The Sporting News, 1983

In our family, nobody eats breakfast. But after noon, the kill is on. We just sit and eat until we go to bed.

Cella Dupree Connors, mother of
Oklahoma running back Marcus
Dupree
Sports Illustrated, 1983

That weightlifting is cute, and they look good in their clothes, but give me a guy who'll go four quarters chewing tobacco.

Dick Bass, Chargers defensive
coordinator

Just another way to get tired.

Bob Bruenig, Cowboys linebacker, on
aerobic dancing
Sport, 1984

Reporter: As a football player, what is your primary weakness?
Perry: Cheeseburgers.

William "The Refrigerator" Perry,
Bears defensive tackle
The Sporting News, 1985

Every night I tell myself, "I'm going to dream about my girl, I'm going to dream about my girl." But it's always ham hocks.

Nate Newton, 320-pound Cowboys
guard
Sports Illustrated, 1989

 EQUIPMENT

Now this dang football is the only game I know of that ain't played with a round ball. Football is gonna bounce on you. Folks are gonna win and folks are gonna lose, and a man's got to be a man about it.

> Abe Martin, Texas Christian coach

The man who complains about the way the ball bounces is likely the one who dropped it.

> Lou Holtz, Arkansas coach
> *Sport,* 1981

Why don't they bring out a ball and give it to the team which doesn't have one? Wouldn't that solve everything?

> George Plimpton, writer and editor,
> quoting an English girl at her first game
> *One More July,* 1977

Do you wonder where all the footballs in the NFL go? Players that make interceptions have them at home.

> John Madden, broadcaster
> "NFL Pre-Season Football," CBS-TV,
> 1983

I want to intercept a pass, run the length of the field, and score a touchdown. Then, instead of spiking the ball, I will squeeze it so hard with my hands that it explodes, and then I will throw the deflated pigskin to the ground.

> Tom Cousineau, Browns linebacker
> *USA Today,* 1984

None of that sissy stuff for me. I just let my hair grow long and pulled it through a turtleneck sweater.

> W. W. "Pudge" Heffelfinger, former
> Yale lineman, on helmets

Why does a player have to wear a facemask that looks as if it's the grillwork from a 1955 Buick?

> Leigh Montville, sportswriter
> *Inside Sports*, 1982

Red is kind of a wimpy color. Maybe next they'll make us wear little flowers on our jerseys, up around the shoulder pads. And then we can have Big Bird on the sides of our pants to make the kids happy.

> Fred Smerlas, Bills offensive tackle,
> on red helmets
> *Sports Illustrated*, 1984

I once thought about playing football but you have to wear too much equipment and people can't see you.

> Muhammad Ali, heavyweight boxer
> *San Francisco Chronicle*, 1978

I could be protected like an armadillo, but then I might play like one.

> Bob Chandler, Raiders receiver
> *Sports Illustrated*, 1982

Reporter: How did you get number 77?
Grange: The guy in front of me got 76; the guy in back got 78.

> Red Grange, former running back
> *Sports Illustrated*, 1985

Numbers show speed. You get in the secondary in zone coverage, and they see 46, they know the guy's a stiff. He's a third-string white guy who can't run. He made the team because he makes tackles on kickoffs.

> Todd Christensen, Raiders tight end,
> on why he likes his number 46
> *USA Today*, 1984

The Raiders aren't sinister. They just have a sinister tailor.

> Dan Fouts, Chargers quarterback
> *San Francisco Chronicle*, 1981

When we get those black shirts on, you can sense the fear on the field. You get those black babies on, you feel baaad!

> Vann McElroy, Raiders safety
> *Gentlemen's Quarterly*, 1984

When they first come out on the field, they're intimidating. But as the game goes on, the color becomes a lot lighter.

> Kellen Winslow, Chargers tight end
> *Inside Sports*, 1981

We want them to look ugly because when you look ugly, you work harder.

> Chuck Noll, Steelers coach, on his
> team's high-top sneakers for indoor
> practice
> *San Francisco Examiner*, 1981

That's good. We have to learn how to play on a wet field, too.

> Duffy Daugherty, Michigan State
> coach, spilling his coffee on play
> diagrams

Momma always told me never to wear a hat indoors. When it can't rain on you, you're indoors.

> Bum Phillips, Oilers coach, on why
> he doesn't wear a hat in the
> Astrodome
> *He Ain't No Bum*, 1980

The injuries are brutal and the fields stink; at the end of the game they smell of vomit and spit and blood because it doesn't go into the earth. All the odors just cook there on this plastic turf.

> Norman Mailer, writer, on artificial
> turf

We think of it as fuzzy concrete.

> John McKay, Southern California
> coach, on artificial turf

It only feels hard when you walk on it.

> Tex Schramm, Cowboys general
> manager, on the artificial turf at
> Texas Stadium, 1972

AstroTurf never bothers us because Larry and I can't make ninety-degree turns. In fact, I don't think we move fast enough to slip.

> Jim Kiick, on his fellow Dolphins
> running back Larry Csonka, 1972

They ought to ban it, get rid of it, or use it as a weapon. They should send all our AstroTurf to El Salvador and kill all the rebels by having them play football on it.

> John Matuszak, Raiders defensive
> end
> *Playboy*, 1982

I hate it. I just do. That, local news, the IRS, and hair dryers are the four worst inventions of this century.

> Beano Cook, football analyst, on
> artificial turf
> *Sport*, 1985

The guy who invented it should be made to sleep on it.

> Jerry Glanville, Oilers offensive
> coordinator, on artificial turf
> *Sports Illustrated*, 1985

My definition of real football is no domes, no plastic turf, no waves, no mayors making bets.

> John Madden, broadcaster
> "NFL Football," CBS-TV, 1985

FAMOUS LAST WORDS

Sometime, Rock, when the team's up against it, when things are wrong and the breaks are beating the boys, ask them to win one for the Gipper. I don't know where I'll be then, Rock, but I'll know about it and I'll be happy.

> George Gipp, Notre Dame halfback,
> his legendary deathbed request to
> coach Knute Rockne, 1920

When autumn comes and the leaves fall off the trees, I'll be on the football field.

> Knute Rockne, 1930. (He died in a
> plane crash March 31, 1931.)

I don't know what's wrong with it. It's worked for forty years.

> Pop Warner, Temple coach, on his
> outmoded pass defense, 1935. (He
> retired soon after this comment.)

If Stanford wins a single game with that crazy formation, you can throw all the football I ever knew into the Pacific Ocean. What Clark is doing is positively ridiculous.

> Pop Warner, former coach, on
> Stanford coach Clark Shaughnessy's
> revolutionary T-formation, 1940.
> (Stanford went 9–0 and was ranked
> second nationally.)

When the other fellow has a thousand dollars and you have a dime is the time to gamble.

> Fritz Crisler, Michigan coach,
> inaugurating the two-platoon system
> against Army, 1945. (Army won
> 28–7.)

You can't do that to my Golden Bears!

> Bud Brennan, California fan who
> tackled Michigan's Tom Harmon on
> his fourth touchdown run in the
> 1940 Rose Bowl, which Michigan
> won 41–0

Coach, he was the only man open.

> Johnny Lujack, Notre Dame
> quarterback, when asked by coach
> Frank Leahy why he threw three
> interceptions to Army's Arnold
> Tucker, 1946

I guess I'm too full of Alabama.

> Tommy Lewis, Alabama fan, after he
> brought down Rice's fullback on his
> way to a ninety-five-yard touchdown
> run in the 1954 Cotton Bowl, which
> Rice won 28–6

We're trying to build a university our football team can be proud of.

> George L. Cross, Oklahoma
> president, to coach Bud Wilkinson

This team of ours is the worst I've ever seen in training. I can't control it. I can't coach it. So I'm quitting. As a matter of fact, I'm leaving Detroit tonight.

> Buddy Parker, Lions coach, a few
> days before the first 1957 exhibition
> game. (The Lions went on to win the
> NFL title without Parker.)

I'll be commissioner when the sun goes down tonight, and I'll be commissioner when the sun comes up Friday.

> Joe Foss, American Football League
> commissioner, who one and a half
> hours later announced his
> resignation, 1966

The New York Jets would do well to trade Joe Namath right now. . . . It is unlikely that the Jets can ever win with Namath and [Coach Weeb] Ewbank out of harmony. . . . One or the other should go.

> William N. Wallace, football analyst,
> *The New York Times*, 1968. (Namath
> and the Jets won the 1969 Super
> Bowl.)

We are confident that if the city acquires Yankee Stadium and completes its plans for modernization of the stadium, the New York Giants will remain in New York City.

> John V. Lindsay, New York
> mayor, 1971. (They moved to New
> Jersey.)

Preempt Doris Day? Are you out of your mind?

> Bob Wood, CBS Network president,
> refusing "Monday Night Football,"
> 1970

When you've got two broken hands with casts on 'em and you go to the men's room, that's where you really find out who your friends are.

> Alex Hawkins, CBS-TV broadcaster,
> when Miami defensive back Jake
> Scott came into the game with two
> broken hands. "That's the last word
> we heard from The Hawk over the
> public airwaves for a long time,"
> wrote George Plimpton.

All right, men. Now I lay me down to sleep, I pray the Lord my soul . . .

> Bill Peterson, Florida State coach,
> leading the wrong pregame prayer

Any company that doesn't let its employees off on Bronco
Day should be ashamed of itself.

> Richard Lamm, Colorado governor,
> declaring a holiday when the Broncos
> beat the Raiders for the AFC
> Championship, 1977. (He later
> backed down upon learning it would
> cost the state over $5 million; Dallas
> beat Denver in the Super Bowl.)

It is extremely doubtful if any coach active today will even
come close to approaching [Amos Alonzo] Stagg's 314 victories.

> Mervin D. Hyman and Gordon S.
> White, Jr., sportswriters, *Big Ten
> Football,* 1977. (Alabama's Bear
> Bryant won his 323rd game in 1982
> before retiring, and Eddie Robinson
> of Grambling State through the 1989
> season had won 358.)

I intend to die at halftime of an Ohio State–Michigan game.

> Woody Hayes, Ohio State coach. (He
> was forced to retire after striking one
> of his players during the 1978 Gator
> Bowl; he died on March 12, 1987.)

The Rams are the same old tough team. They are sprinkled
with Pro Bowlers. . . . They are very, very talented and
much better than the 49ers.

> Tom Landry, Cowboys coach,
> October 1981. (The 49ers finished
> 13–3 and won the Super Bowl; the
> Rams record was 6–10.)

I'd like my son to grow up to be just like Billy Kilmer.

> Tom Brookshier, broadcaster, the day
> after the Redskins quarterback was
> arrested for drunken driving
> "NFL Football," CBS-TV, 1981

What a finish for John Elway, to pull this out. This is one of
the great finishes. Only a miracle can save the Bears.

> Joe Starkey, broadcaster, KGO-Radio,
> San Francisco, just before the five-
> lateral kickoff return that Kevin
> Moen of Calilfornia ran through the
> Stanford band to defeat Stanford
> 25–20, 1983

He'll never be any good.

> Robert Irsay, Colts owner, upon
> sending quarterback John Elway to
> the Broncos, 1983. (Elway led
> Denver to the AFC West title that
> year with an 11–5 record and to AFC
> championships in 1986, 1987, and
> 1989.)

[Redskins coach Joe] Gibbs wanted to get this kid, and that
little monkey gets loose, doesn't he?

> Howard Cosell, "Monday Night
> Football," ABC-TV, 1983, on the
> Redskins Alvin Garrett. (Cosell was
> roundly criticized for this comment
> on the five-foot-seven black receiver.)

Quit coaching? I'd croak in a week.

> Bear Bryant, Alabama coach, oft-
> quoted comment. (He announced his
> retirement on December 14, 1982,
> won the Liberty Bowl on December
> 26, and died of a heart attack January
> 26, 1983.)

What lies behind us and what lies before us are small mat-
ters compared to what lies within us.

> Monte Clark, Lions coach, quoting
> Ralph Waldo Emerson after a 4–11–
> 1 season, 1984. (Three days later, he
> was fired.)

I know it's the American way to say you always have a chance, but it's also the American way not to lie.

> Jim Walden, Iowa State coach, before
> Oklahoma beat his team 56–3, 1987

For years people called us the armpit of the San Gabriel Valley. Today we're the crown jewel.

> Xavier Hermosillo, mayor of
> Irwindale, California, where the
> Raiders announced they would move,
> 1987. (They didn't.)

I will not let it happen again. That wasn't me.

> Stan Parrish, Kansas State coach,
> after his team went 0–10–1, 1987.
> (They went 0–11 the next year.)

I thought this might be a great team, but now we'll have to fight and struggle just to compete.

> Lou Holtz, Notre Dame coach, 1989.
> (His team finished 11–1 and ranked
> number two.)

 **FANS AND ALUMNI**

I keep dummies on the field to make the alumni happy.

> Bob Zuppke, Illinois coach, on
> tackling dummies

I won't know until my barber tells me on Monday.

> Knute Rockne, Notre Dame coach,
> when asked why he lost

An atheist is a guy who watches a Notre Dame–Southern Methodist game and doesn't care who wins.

> Dwight D. Eisenhower

Society needs no replacement for the football coach. What it should try to achieve is a system for getting rid of alumni.

> Forrest Evashevski, Iowa coach, 1952

One time they gave me a standing boo ovation at Kezar Stadium. Those fans always gave me 100 percent.

> George Halas, Bears coach

Whatever else might be said about [President Richard M.] Nixon—and there is still serious doubt in my mind he could pass for human—he is a goddamn stone fanatic on every facet of pro football.

> Hunter S. Thompson, writer
> *Fear and Loathing on the Campaign*
> *Trail '72,* 1973

How could Nixon know so little about Watergate and so much about football?

> Joe Paterno, Penn State coach,
> commencement address, 1974

I left because of illness and fatigue. The fans were sick and tired of me.

> John Ralston, former Broncos coach

You know what a football fan is, don't you? That's a guy who sits forty rows up in the stands and wonders why a seventeen-year-old kid can't hit another seventeen-year-old kid with a ball forty yards away. . . . Then he goes out to the parking lot and can't find his car.

> Chuck Mills, Wake Forest coach

Any wife whose husband watches more than five football games in one weekend should be able to have him declared legally dead.

> Johnny Carson
> "The Tonight Show," NBC-TV, 1979

It sometimes bothers me that people are out there yelling for my head. I wouldn't boo one of those fans if he came to my house and did a lousy job on the plumbing.

> Pat Haden, Rams quarterback, 1979

They booed me the first time I was introduced. I think they followed me from Houston.

> Dan Pastorini, Raiders quarterback
> traded from Houston, 1980

If you're sitting in the end zone and your team is driving toward you, the quarter will end when your team is on the three-yard line.

> Glenn Dickey, sports columnist
> *San Francisco Chronicle*, 1981

Fans sometimes don't understand it. The other team gets paid, too.

> Fran Tarkenton, broadcaster
> "Monday Night Football," ABC-TV,
> 1981

Dallas fans never feel the Cowboys have lost a game. It's always that the referees screwed 'em or the good Lord looked the other way or something.

> Tom Brookshier, CBS-TV broadcaster
> *Sports Illustrated*, 1982

One of the delights about being in broadcasting is that fans rarely boo the announcers.

> Pat Haden, broadcaster and former
> quarterback
> *San Francisco Examiner*, 1982

I got a letter two weeks ago from a guy in Tulsa bad-mouthing me. He even had his return address on it. What's the matter with some people, anyway?

> Turner Gill, Nebraska quarterback
> *Sports Illustrated*, 1982

You wouldn't think people would have much time for that. I don't even have time to write people I like.

Mark Cooper, Broncos offensive
tackle, on hate mail
Sports Illustrated, 1983

Remember, it takes a woman nine months to have a baby, no matter how many men you put in the job.

Lou Holtz, University of Minnesota
coach, reminding fans that a team
needs time to develop
Life, 1984

I'm getting tired of scraping vegetables off my car. And I didn't like it when they shaved my girlfriend's head.

Russ Francis, 49ers tight end, on
rough fans
The Sporting News, 1985

Look at those guys. They must be mentally retarded. I bet their parents were cousins.

Tuffy Knight, Toronto Argonauts
executive, reacting to fans taking
their shirts off when it was thirty
below zero, 1985

That's why you are seeing more coaches go into the cattle business—because cattle don't have alumni.

Earle Bruce, Ohio State coach
Sports Illustrated, 1986

The NFL likes to think of itself as providing entertainment for the corporate set, for guys who go to work in three-piece suits but who show up at the stadium disguised in sweatshirts and Levis.

Conrad Dobler, former guard
They Call Me Dirty, 1988

This is preseason, when the only noise you usually hear is fans griping about ticket prices.

Gary Shelton, sportswriter, 1989

FOOTBALL: THE GAME

A game that can keep you young and vibrant and all
steamed up is a precious thing.

> W. W. "Pudge" Heffelfinger, former
> Yale lineman

Football was invented by a mean son of a bitch, and that's
the way the game's supposed to be played.

> Steve Owen, Giants coach, 1940s

The story of dangers avoided and obstacles surmounted is
one of which we never tire. The American game of football
is such a story constantly enacted before our eyes. Its great
protagonists are not easily forgotten.

> Paul Gallico, sportswriter

Dahling, mink is for football games.

> Tallulah Bankhead, actress, when
> asked why she wore velvet instead of
> mink

I was a lousy football player, but I remember Chief New-
man, our coach, saying that "There's one thing about
Nixon, he plays every scrimmage as though the championship were at stake."

> Richard M. Nixon, Vice President, on
> Whittier College
> *Saturday Evening Post*, 1958

Thinking in football terms may be the best way to understand what finally happened with the whole Watergate
thing. Coach Nixon's team is fourth and thirty-two on their own

ten, and he finds out that his punter is a junkie. A sick junkie.

Hunter S. Thompson, writer
Playboy, 1974

I don't think Richard Nixon would make a good coach because he'd be in trouble with the NCAA all the time.

Billy Tubbs, Oklahoma basketball
coach
"The Lighter Side of Sports," ESPN-
TV, 1989

Pro football is like nuclear warfare. There are no winners, only survivors.

Frank Gifford, Giants running back
Sports Illustrated, 1960

This is a game for madmen. In football we're all mad.

Vince Lombardi, Packers coach

Football today is far too much a sport for the few who can play it well; the rest of us, and too many of our children, get our exercise from climbing up the seats of the stadium or from walking across the room to turn on our television sets.

John F. Kennedy, speech, 1961

It is, in fact, the intellectual's secret vice. Not politics, not sex, not pornography, but football, and not college football but the real thing. Pro ball is the opium of the intellectuals.

William Phillips, political writer
Commentary

Football is a game designed to keep coal miners off the streets.

Jimmy Breslin, columnist, 1973

To me football is like a day off. I grew up picking cotton on my daddy's farm, and nobody asked for your autograph or put your name in the paper for that.

Lee Roy Jordan, Cowboys linebacker

Football compels us primarily with its explosive choreography, its terse blend of skill pirouetting on a field mined with danger. It is a game of action that must be seen to be enjoyed.

Larry Merchant, sportswriter
The National Football Lottery, 1973

Gene Hackman: For them that don't have football, there's always religion.

Night Moves (film), 1975
Screenplay by Alan Sharp

The football player himself seems a kind of a natural descendant from the mythical tall-in-the-saddle Texan, that threefold blend of physical machismo, psychic masochism, and Calvinist certitude.

Al Reinert, writer
Atlantic Monthly, 1975

Both games are great. The colleges have all the leaves turning brown, and we've got the girls with the big chests.

John McKay, Buccaneers coach

It's a very interesting game. They have big bears up front and little rabbits in the back. The idea is for the bears to protect the rabbits.

Viktor Tikonov, Soviet hockey coach,
1976

Please don't take this in a facetious way—our teaching of football is excellent. The indication of this is that children who want to be good football players don't complain that the work is too hard.

Edward Teller, physicist
Playboy, 1979

Southern football is a religion, emanating direly from its be-deviled landscape and the burden of the past.

> Willie Morris, writer
> *Inside Sports,* 1980

America's right-wing guerrilla theater.

> Don Meredith, former Cowboys
> quarterback
> *Inside Sports,* 1980

Football is itself the biggest dramatization of American busi-ness ever invented.

> Marshall McLuhan, Canadian
> educator and author
> *Inside Sports,* 1981

It's almost like life. Just when it begins to look rosy, some-body will intercept a pass and run ninety yards against you.

> John Facenda, NFL Films narrator
> *Sport,* 1982

They're so friendly. When they hit each other, they pat each other on the buns. But I think it's a bit over the top, all those guys hugging and kissing each other after the score.

> Cera Wynne, Londoner, after
> watching the Cardinals play
> the Vikings in Wembley
> Stadium
> *The Sporting News,* 1983

You could invent a cure for cancer and some people would still think, "Yeah, but you didn't play professional football."

> Frank Champi, former Harvard
> quarterback who didn't play
> professional football
> *Inside Sports,* 1983

In the East, football is a cultural experience. In the West, it is a form of tourism. In the Midwest, it is a form of cannibalism. But in the South, football is a religion, and Saturday is a holy day of obligation.

> Marino Casem, Alcorn State coach,
> 1983

There is only one American sport. It involves a pig bladder, huge stadiums of seventy thousand spectators, and medieval violence and costumes. It is presented with slo-mo, reverse angles, and an eye in the sky.

> C. W. Nevius, sportswriter
> *San Francisco Chronicle,* 1984

I like football pretty much. It's the commercialism I don't like. The day will come when the star quarterback will sell Tampax. It's only a matter of time.

> Rita Mae Brown, novelist
> *San Francisco Chronicle,* 1985

Football combines two grim features of American life, violence and committee meetings [huddles].

> George F. Will, writer
> *Newsweek,* 1985

The thing I like about football is that you don't have to take a shower before you go to work.

> Jay Hilgenberg, Bears center, 1985

I'm pretty excited today—only fifty-six weeks to go before the USFL season starts.

> David Letterman
> "Late Night with David Letterman,"
> NBC-TV, 1986

Football is great. You get to kick, bite, sweat, spit, fight, win, and afterward hug a blonde.

> Kyle Rappold, Colorado nose tackle,
> 1987

FOOTBALL AND OTHER ACTIVITIES

At least in the ring you know what you are doing. You know what you're opponent is trying to do. He's right there in front of you. There's only one of him. But in football, dammit, there's eleven guys trying to do you in!

> John L. Sullivan, former heavyweight
> boxer

Spahn throws a baseball, and some other guy hits it with a bat. I throw a football, and right after that a lot of guys weighing 250 pounds hit me.

> Y. A. Tittle, Giants quarterback

If I was going to get beat up, I wanted to be indoors where it was warm.

> Tom Heinsohn, basketball forward

Being in politics is like being a football coach. You have to be smart enough to understand the game and dumb enough to think it's important.

> Eugene McCarthy, presidential
> candidate, 1968

The TV football widow said to her husband, "You love football more than me." He said, "Yes, but I love you more than basketball."

> Jerry Kramer, former Packers guard
> *Sports Illustrated*, 1972

Sleep is all the recreation you need.

> George Allen, Redskins coach

The world's greatest optimists are fishermen and football players. Only they don't always make the big catch.

Norm Evans, offensive tackle
On the Line, 1976

Baseball is easy to fathom, not like football, which people explain to me at great length and I understand for one brief moment before it all falls apart in my brain and looks like an ominous calculus problem.

Eve Babitz, writer
Slow Days, Fast Company, 1977

I'd rather be a football coach. That way you only lose eleven games a year.

Abe Lemons, Texas basketball coach

You either have to finesse twelve people who weren't smart enough to get out of jury duty, or eleven who weren't smart enough to play offense.

Steve Fuller, Clemson quarterback,
on the difference between law and
football, 1979

When I went to a Catholic high school in Philadelphia, we just had one coach for football and basketball. He took all of us who turned out and had us run through a forest. The ones who ran into trees went on the football team.

George Raveling, basketball coach
San Francisco Examiner, 1980

I played other games, too. I know of no other game that gave me the same feeling that football did. Football went deeper. That's why you can look at that bench when the TV camera comes over and see the fellows sitting there crying. I've sat there crying.

Ronald W. Reagan
Inside Sports, 1981

The only difference between chess and football is before I was directing the pieces and now I'm one of them.

Kellen Winslow, Chargers receiver
San Francisco Chronicle, 1982

I didn't like the idea of practicing six days to play one.

Robin Yount, baseball shortstop
Sports Illustrated, 1982

How many girls can tell you the name of a college baseball star?

Eric Dickerson, Rams running back,
on why he chose football
San Francisco Examiner, 1983

It's a very plastic world. It's fake, a lot of makeup and phony people. It's a world of illusion, a dream world, and it's hard to get in—kind of like football.

Hosea Fortune, Chargers receiver, on
modeling
The Sporting News, 1983

There was very little sports in the news over there. Everyone was worried about survival, not who's in first place.

George Perles, Michigan State coach,
on Asia
Seattle Post-Intelligencer, 1985

I have never been around so many crummy people in all my days.

Ed "Too Tall" Jones, Cowboys
defensive lineman, on his boxing
career
Los Angeles Times, 1986

When the field gets muddy in baseball, they stop the game. When the field gets muddy in football, the players roll around in it like boar hogs.

Ira Berkow, sportswriter
The New York Times, 1986

I enjoy the many [golf] tournaments I play in where we so-called celebrities are teamed with businessmen. . . . You never know when you're going to need a parking ticket fixed.

Jim McMahon, Bears quarterback
McMahon, 1987

I love football. Football is something I can sleep with. Baseball is just a hot date.

Deion Sanders, Falcons defensive
back and baseball prospect
San Francisco Chronicle, 1989

 **GREAT RIVALRIES**

Players, students, mothers, and daddies—they all know each other because they grew up around here together. They're all our friends, and nobody can hate you like your friends.

John McKay, Southern California
coach, on UCLA, 1965

Every fan has *somebody* he likes to see beaten. . . . Turn a UCLA man around three times, and he'll stagger straight to the USC campus with a couple of buckets of blue and gold paint.

Dan Jenkins, sportswriter
Saturday's America, 1970

A contest that is college football's equivalent of a prison riot—with coeds.

Dan Jenkins, on Oklahoma versus
Texas
Saturday's America, 1970

Why, that's just like somebody from the United States playing for Nazi Germany.

> Harold Philipp, Texas fullback, on
> Texas natives playing for Oklahoma

I don't buy one goddamn drop of gas in the state of Michigan! We'll coast and *push* this goddamn car to Ohio before I give this state a nickel of my money.

> Woody Hayes, Ohio State coach to
> assistant Ed Ferkany

Woody Hayes' complete dislike of anything relevant to the state of Michigan is almost legendary in Ohio. He will not even mention the Michigan team by name. It is only "that team up north."

> Jerry Brondfield, writer and editor
> *Woody Hayes and the 100-Yard War,*
> 1974

We don't want to be intimidated at Michigan. That's what happens to three quarters of the teams that go up there and play before 103,000 people. Heck, we don't have that many hogs here in Iowa.

> Hayden Fry, Iowa coach, 1981

It's a football game, so important that it's called The Game. There is no other The Game.

> George Plimpton, writer and editor,
> on Harvard versus Yale
> *Sports Illustrated,* 1981

I'd rather lose and live in Provo than win and live in Laramie.

> LaVell Edwards, Brigham Young
> coach, after losing to Wyoming in a
> snowstorm
> *Sports Illustrated,* 1981

Before I die, I want to sit in the stands and watch an SC–
Notre Dame game.

> John McKay, former Southern
> California coach
> *Inside Sports,* 1982

There are four important stages in your life. You're born,
you play the Huskies, you get married, and you die.

> Dan Lynch, Washington State guard,
> on the University of Washington
> *Seattle Post-Intelligencer,* 1984

This is called "Texas-OU Weekend." The object is to puke
on the Adolphus Hotel so many times that a guy in a monkey suit comes out and takes you to jail and then you don't
have to drive over to the Cotton Bowl the next day and get
your antenna twisted into a balloon animal by a car parker
from Iraq who's been pouring asphalt on his front yard.

> "Joe Bob Briggs," a.k.a. John Bloom,
> columnist, on Texas versus
> Oklahoma
> *Dallas Times-Herald,* 1984

HEAVY HITTING

In short, in life, as in a football game, the principle to follow
is: Hit the line hard; don't foul and don't shirk, but hit the
line hard.

> Theodore Roosevelt
> *The Strenuous Life,* 1910

You've got to play football for all there's in it or somebody
who hits harder will send you off on a stretcher.

> W. W. "Pudge" Heffelfinger, former
> Yale lineman

Dancing is a contact sport. Football is a hitting sport.

> Bob Zuppke, Illinois coach

I always go straight for the head. Whoever's across from me, I bash him with the flat part of my hand—nail him square on the ear hole of his helmet about five straight times. Pretty soon he gets so nervous he can't concentrate. He can't even hear the signals. Once I get him spooked, the rest is easy.

> Gene "Big Daddy" Lipscomb,
> defensive tackle

Christ, I can't think of any plays.

> Y. A. Tittle, Giants quarterback, after
> getting hit by Lions defensive back
> Dick "Night Train" Lane, 1962

Anybody who says this game is beastly, brutal, and nasty, he's right.

> Wayne Walker, Lions linebacker

When I get to the man with the ball, I hit him as hard as I can. If I can hit a man hard enough so he has to be carried off the field, I'll be glad to help him off.

> Deacon Jones, Rams defensive end

I'm going to hit him. I'm going to let him know I'm still around. I want him to remember Ray Nitschke even in his dreams.

> Ray Nitschke, former Packers
> linebacker
> *Mean on Sunday,* 1973

Our kids are never brutal. Of course, that opposing quarterback better be careful about running a whole lot.

> Woody Hayes, Ohio State coach

I never saw a man make a tackle with a smile on his face.
You just don't laugh your way to victory.

> Woody Hayes, 1976

It's not a normal thing to run down the field and run into
somebody. You have to convince yourself that that's the
thing to do.

> Chuck Noll, Steelers coach

You know, Joe, if you wouldn't keep jumping in the air, I
wouldn't keep punching you in the stomach.

> Conrad Dobler, Cardinals guard,
> when "Mean Joe" Greene kept
> leaping to bat down passes

Americans love football because they like seeing somebody
getting knocked on his butt. . . . It's not barbaric. Fans just
love to see someone get boned.

> Tom Cousineau, Browns linebacker
> *Sports Illustrated,* 1979

We had a defensive coach at Ohio State who used to tell us:
"If a man comes over the middle and catches a pass, make
a snot bubble." Hit him so hard that a snot bubble comes
out of his nose. Coaches get pretty colorful in the locker
room.

> Jack Tatum, Raiders defensive back
> *Inside Sports,* 1980

The football field is no place to say I'm sorry.

> Mike Davis, Raiders safety
> *San Francisco Chronicle,* 1981

I don't concentrate on intimidating them so much as I concentrate on kicking their ass.

> John Matuszak, Raiders defensive
> end
> *Playboy,* 1981

I'm 177 pounds. To me, they all hit hard.

> Renaldo Nehemiah, 49ers receiver
> *Sports Illustrated*, 1982

Letterman: Did you ever do anything dirty or untoward?
Donovan: Absolutely.

> Art Donovan, former Colts defensive
> tackle
> "Late Night with David Letterman,"
> NBC-TV, 1983

I went into a game with two goals: one, just to try to knock somebody into next week, and two, just to make sure they weren't looking when I did it.

> Doug Plank, former Bears safety,
> 1986

I don't pick on anybody who has a number above 30.

> Mike Ditka, Bears coach
> *Sports Illustrated*, 1986

I'm an artist. Only my art is to assault people.

> Howie Long, Raiders defensive end
> *People*, 1986

HIGH TIMES

When it's third and ten, you can take the milk drinkers and I'll take the whiskey drinkers every time.

> Max McGee, Packers receiver

The stuff's damn good, even without Scotch in it.

> Max McGee, on the water at practice

When you're up at that time of the night, it's tough enough getting up a game, much less screening the applicants.

> Alex Hawkins, Colts halfback, after
> getting arrested in an early-morning
> poker game with a man who had
> been arrested thirty-three times

Currie: Hey, Ray, what's it like, not drinking?
Nitschke: It's quiet, man. Real quiet.

> Ray Nitschke, Packers linebacker, to
> teammate Dan Currie

Pads? Cookie didn't need pads. Just a helmet and enough bennies to fill the palm of one hand.

> Larry Grantham, Jets linebacker, on
> teammate, running back Cookie
> Gilchrist

I like my girls blonde and my Johnnie Walker red.

> Joe Namath, Jets quarterback
> *I Can't Wait Until Tomorrow . . . ,*
> 1969

If Pete Rozelle, the commissioner, put a lock on the pill bottle, half the players would fall asleep in the third quarter.

> Chip Oliver, former Raiders
> linebacker
> *High for the Game,* 1971

I would really, truly like to run out of money and breath in the same hour. If they could put it in a computer now and tell me when, we could really get it on.

> Bobby Layne, former Lions
> quarterback

Some people needed ten hours' sleep. I needed four. Mr. Edison didn't sleep but two hours a night.

> Bobby Layne

All the independence I really need in a woman is the ability to drive a pickup truck so we can get home if I happen to pass out.

> Ken Stabler, Oilers quarterback
> *Inside Sports,* 1980

I'm a Scotch drinker. Just like Joe Namath. Sonny Jurgensen drinks Scotch. Hell, so does Tom Flores. Maybe all great quarterbacks drink Scotch. I drink it any way I can get it . . . with ice, without ice, with water, with soda. It doesn't make any difference. I'll drink it straight from the bottle.

> Ken Stabler

Nick Nolte, getting a shot in the knee: Better football through chemistry, huh?

> *North Dallas Forty* (film), 1979
> Screenplay by Frank Yablans, Ted
> Kotcheff, and Peter Gent

I'm glad the bars close at 1 A.M. here. If I'd been drafted by New York, I'd be dead.

> Tommy Kramer, Vikings quarterback
> *Inside Sports,* 1981

That's like saying you're robbing a bank for fun.

> Bum Phillips, Saints coach, on using
> cocaine "for recreation"
> *The Sporting News,* 1982

They're bringing football players and racehorses really close together. Next, they'll want to put us on a block, look at our teeth, and brand our arms.

> Dan Dierdorf, Cardinals offensive
> tackle, on urine testing
> *Sports Illustrated,* 1982

I'll stay out of bars when women cease to go in.

John Matuszak, Raiders defensive
end
The Sporting News, 1982

If they want to test me like Foolish Pleasure or Secretariat, then pay me like that.

Jerry Robinson, Eagles linebacker,
1982

I'd have them taken off to the public square and hung by the neck till the wind whistled through their bones.

Jack Lambert, Steelers linebacker, on
drug dealers
Sport, 1982

I found myself past the point of doing drugs. Drugs were doing me.

Thomas "Hollywood" Henderson,
former linebacker, on his cocaine
habit
Denver Post, 1983

It's big in the USFL because if you don't make it here, you're thrown right out into the real world.

Jim Byrne, New Jersey Generals
defensive end, on steroids
Sports Illustrated, 1985

I used to think you needed to be hung over to play in the NFL.

John Riggins, Redskins fullback
Riggins in Motion, 1985

They didn't mind after they learned they didn't have to study for them.

Mack Brown, Tulane coach, on his
players' reaction to drug testing, 1986

This guy was arrested for selling "clean urine" to pass a drug test. This was his defense: "Hey, I just sell the stuff. I don't know what people do with it."

> Jay Leno, comedian
> "Late Night with David Letterman,"
> NBC-TV, 1987

An ex-FBI agent working in the league office gave a powerful lecture about the physical and legal consequences of drug abuse. Unfortunately, at a cocktail party after the lecture, he got drunk and fell into the salad bowl.

> Gene Klein, former Chargers owner
> *First Down and a Billion*, 1987

He's the only person I know who can down fifty beers without having to stop once to take a leak.

> Conrad Dobler, retired guard, on
> former Cardinals coach Jim Hanifan
> *They Call Me Dirty*, 1988

This is the first time in the history of labor negotiations that $100,000 players are driving Mark IVs or Cadillacs to the picket line.

> Joe Robbie, Dolphins owner, on the
> NFL Players Association strike
> *The New York Times*, 1974

Outlined against a pile of legal briefs, the Four Horsemen rode into the 1982 NFL season: Labor unrest, drugs, personnel raids, and Congress.

> Paul Zimmerman, football analyst
> *Sports Illustrated*, 1982

News that a strike of football players might wipe out the entire football season left me positively pleased. Didn't we just have a football season a few weeks ago?

Russell Baker, columnist
The New York Times, 1982

If we do strike, you know who'll settle it? The wives.

Ahmad Rashad, Vikings receiver
Sports Illustrated, 1982

I miss football, even the interceptions.

Archie Manning, Oilers quarterback
Sports Illustrated, 1982

I don't let my wife eat anymore. And I fired the maids and butler. We also put off buying storm windows.

Gordon King, Giants offensive tackle
San Francisco Examiner, 1982

I'm a little worried about the bookies. If the thing lasts, some of them might have to take their kids out of Harvard.

Beano Cook, football analyst
New York *Daily News,* 1982

The most significant thing that came out of it was that they told us not to steal the ashtrays.

Doug Dieken, Browns player
representative, on meetings with the
commissioner's office
Sports Illustrated, 1982

The best description of "utter waste" would be a busload of lawyers to go over a cliff with three empty seats.

Lamar Hunt, Chiefs owner
San Francisco Examiner, 1982

Jack Donlan has done the job of three men—Larry, Curly, and Moe.

Eddie Payton, Vikings running back,
on the chief negotiator for the NFL
San Francisco Examiner, 1982

One good thing came out of the strike: My wife's pregnant.

> Matt Cavanaugh, Patriots
> quarterback
> *San Francisco Examiner*, 1982

I told his agent if Leon didn't get to camp soon, he wouldn't be Dr. Sack, he'd be Dr. Bench.

> Marv Levy, Bills coach, on defensive
> end Leon "Dr. Sack" Seals, 1987

Is it just me, or does it seem that the NFL season has just flown by this year?

> David Letterman, on the strike after
> Week Two
> "Late Night with David Letterman,"
> NBC-TV, 1987

It's not like you're getting them out of a tavern somewhere. Okay, we got some out of a tavern.

> John Robinson, Rams coach, on the
> replacement players, 1987

We are the official Washington Redskins. We represent the entire state of Washington.

> Charles Jackson, Redskins
> replacement defensive back, 1987

Without the players, [NFL Players Representative Ed] Garvey contended, there would be no professional football. Of course, the same thing could be said about the footballs.

> Gene Klein, former Chargers owner
> *First Down and a Billion*, 1987

TOP TEN SCAB SLOGANS OF THE SCAB NFL:

10. We're not football players, but we play them on TV!
 9. Come for the refund—stay for the game!
 8. Bring a helmet and join the fun!
 7. Get spit on by Lawrence Taylor!

6. It still beats Arena Football!
5. Out-of-condition athletes guarantee plenty of injuries!
4. We have a fine selection of magazines!
3. Look! It's my old gym teacher!
2. Enough beer and you won't know the difference!
1. It's scab-tastic!

David Letterman
"Late Night with David Letterman,"
NBC-TV, 1987

TOP TEN NFL STRIKE DEMANDS:

10. Players can smoke on field during point-after attempts.
9. More endive in salad at pre-game brunches.
8. Looser cups.
7. Option to skip locker room pep talk to watch "Up with People" halftime show.
6. Jimmy the Greek must stop wearing K-Mart cologne.
5. No team mascot may be a giant intestinal parasite.
4. Elaborate running plays should be eligible for Tony nominations.
3. Tighter cups.
2. More singalongs in huddle.
1. Random urine testing of Brent Musburger.

David Letterman
"Late Night with David Letterman,"
NBC-TV, 1987

 **LINEBACKERS**

To me, skill is us guys who can run down those fast sons of bitches.

Sam Huff, Giants linebacker

If every college football team had a linebacker like Tommy Nobis [of Texas] or Dick Butkus of Illinois, then surely all

fullbacks were destined to wind up being three feet tall and
singing soprano.

Dan Jenkins, sportswriter
Saturday's America, 1970

Each time I tackled somebody, I tried to make sure that
when he got up and walked away he'd remember he'd met
Ray Nitschke. And I don't mean socially.

Ray Nitschke, Packers linebacker
Mean on Sunday, 1973

Wipe that smile off your face, you chickenshit son of a
bitch.

Dick Butkus, Bears linebacker,
terrifying 49ers quarterback John
Brodie

Look at those eyes. Linebackers have different eyes.

John Madden, broadcaster, on Jack
Youngblood of the Rams
"NFL Football," CBS-TV, 1981

I don't think I'd have enough guts to run into myself.

Harry Carson, Giants linebacker
Sport, 1981

I can run with anyone for eight yards.

Jack Reynolds, 49ers linebacker,
1981

Linebackers are the strangest guys of all. . . . They're people
who just plain love to run into things. They'll hit you as you
go by them the way other people shake hands.

Ahmad Rashad, Vikings receiver
Sports Illustrated, 1982

There's nothing better in life than a head-on collision.

Lawrence Taylor, Giants linebacker
Sport, 1982

Being a middle linebacker is like walking through a lion's cage with a three-piece pork-chop suit on.

> Cecil Johnson, Buccaneers middle
> linebacker
> *Sports Illustrated,* 1982

He has the shortest fuse of any player I've ever coached. He'll strike anything that quivers twice.

> Jim Dickey, Kansas State coach, on
> linebacker Dan Ruzich
> *Sports Illustrated,* 1982

An outside linebacker is like a great gymnast in the Olympics, except that when he comes out of his floor exercise someone's gonna punch him in the teeth.

> Art Rooney, Jr., Steelers head of
> personnel
> *Sports Illustrated,* 1985

He now stands six-foot-four, weighs 245, and runs the forty in 4.5 seconds, which, in the opinion of some, should require him to register his body with the Texas division of motor vehicles.

> Austin Murphy, on Baylor linebacker
> James Francis
> *Sports Illustrated,* 1989

KIM BOKAMPER—Dolphins 1977–1985

He always looks like he's about to slap a waitress.

> Doug Betters, Dolphins defensive end
> *San Francisco Examiner,* 1983

BRIAN BOSWORTH—Seahawks 1987–

He rattled me one time. I didn't see stars, but I saw polka dots.

> Doug DuBose, Nebraska running
> back
> *San Francisco Chronicle,* 1987

It's a good thing Brian was a third child, or he would have been the only one.

Kathy Bosworth, Brian's mother
Sports Illustrated, 1987

I don't think I can compare myself with someone like Bosworth. I mean, who wants to be an idiot?

Jeff Bregel, 49ers guard
The Seattle Times, 1988

The Boz is not an alter ego; it is a commodity, packaged and promoted like beer or deodorant.

Fred Moody, sportswriter
Fighting Chance, 1989

DICK BUTKUS—BEARS 1965–1973

He told the referees they didn't know what they were doing and just picked up the ball after a running play and moved it back. . . . I remember thinking, "If the refs are intimidated by this guy, I'd better be."

Calvin Hill, Browns fullback
Sports Illustrated, 1980

On the sound track of the Bears films, Butkus—when he's going after somebody—sounds like a lion chewing on a big hunk of meat.

Doug Plank, Bears safety

TOM COUSINEAU—MONTREAL ALOUETTES (CFL), BROWNS, AND 49ERS 1979–1987

Yeah, Cousineau played great, but you realize he'll never play as well as his salary. Nobody'll ever play that good.

Sam Rutigliano, Browns coach

BUDDY CURRY—Falcons 1980–1987

This guy was one of the great bullshit artists ever. I mean, he could bullshit his way through a minefield blindfolded and walking on his hands.

> Lawrence Taylor, Giants linebacker
> *LT: Living on the Edge*, 1987

MIKE CURTIS—Colts, Seahawks, and Redskins 1965–1978

Curtis: I'm hustling my ass off.
McCafferty: Well, then, would you hit someone when you get there, please.

> Don McCafferty, Colts coach, 1972

Mike Curtis, the old Colts linebacker, was nicknamed "The Animal." Even the home fans booed him.

> Paul Zimmerman, football analyst
> *The New Thinking Man's Guide to
> Pro Football*, 1984

HUGH GREEN—Buccaneers and Dolphins 1981–

Bill, if you think the guy's so f---ing good, why didn't you draft him?

> Lawrence Taylor, Giants linebacker,
> to Giants coach Bill Parcells, who was
> praising Green, 1981

THOMAS "HOLLYWOOD" HENDERSON— Cowboys, 49ers, and Oilers 1975–1980

On Thomas's list of priorities [winning] ranked somewhere below sex and drugs.

> Harvey Martin, former Cowboys
> defensive end
> *Texas Thunder*, 1986

TED HENDRICKS—COLTS, PACKERS, AND RAIDERS 1969–1983

Secretary: Mr. Davis, Ted Hendricks is on the phone.
Davis: Keep him on the line. At least we know where he is.

> Al Davis, Raiders managing general
> partner, 1977

How many guys come to practice on Halloween wearing a pumpkin on their head with a black stripe and number 83 on it? For Teddy's sake I hope there's a Hall of Fame on Jupiter or Mars.

> Lyle Alzado, Raiders defensive
> lineman
> *Sport,* 1983

When God made Teddy, the button got stuck on fast forward.

> John Matuszak, former defensive
> lineman
> *Cruisin' with the Tooz,* 1987

SAM HUFF—GIANTS AND REDSKINS 1956–1969

Huff didn't say nothing, but he should have kissed me, he was on top of me so much.

> Jim Taylor, Packers fullback, after his
> battle with Huff in the NFL
> Championship Game, 1962

TOM JACKSON—BRONCOS 1973–1986

Jackson is always an inspiration. He even gets fired up for team meetings.

> Karl Mecklenburg, Broncos defensive
> lineman
> *Newsweek,* 1984

CECIL JOHNSON—Buccaneers 1977–1985

He's not the craziest person I know, but he's definitely in the play-offs.

Dave Logan, Buccaneers defensive
tackle
Sports Illustrated, 1982

LEE ROY JORDAN—Cowboys 1963–1976

Toward the end of his career he actually said something nice to me, and that's when I knew he was getting old.

Len Hauss, former Redskins center

JACK LAMBERT—Steelers 1974–1984

This is a crazy world. About the only thing you can depend on in this day and age is a good Lambert hit on Sunday.

Pete Axthelm, sportswriter
Inside Sports, 1981

WILLIE LANIER—Chiefs 1967–1977

It's bad enough playing against a grizzly, but when he's a smart grizzly, too, you've got a problem.

Larry Csonka, Dolphins fullback,
1971

One moment I was planning a move past Lanier, and the next I was knocked out cold.

Ahmad Rashad,
former Vikings receiver
Rashad, 1988

ROD MARTIN—Raiders 1977–1988

Has the thickest hands I've ever seen. Like shaking hands with a cow. . . . Mean? My God, he even scares me sometimes.

Lyle Alzado,
Raiders defensive lineman
Sport, 1983

KARL MECKLENBURG—Broncos 1983–

He's like a cheetah chasing meat.

Myrel Moore,
Broncos linebacker coach, 1986

MATT MILLEN—Raiders and 49ers 1977–

Matt Millen is probably our quietest player off the field, but
the night before a game he gets so wound up that he jumps
off the television set in the hotel room because he thinks
that will bring him good luck.

Lyle Alzado,
Raiders defensive lineman
Sports Illustrated, 1983

RAY NITSCHKE—Packers 1958–1972

I had more fear looking across the line of scrimmage and
seeing Ray Nitschke inches from my nose.

Y. A. Tittle, former quarterback, on a
hunting expedition in New Guinea
Sports Illustrated, 1983

TOMMY NOBIS—Falcons 1966–1976

Tommy is one of those people who is really sort of unhappy
unless he's tackling somebody.

Marvin Kristynik, Texas quarterback

DAVE ROBINSON—Packers and Redskins 1963–1974

Robby will argue any side of any question, just for practice.
I once heard him argue for half an hour that black-eyed
peas are really black-eyed beans. Maybe they are, but who
cares?

Jerry Kramer, Packers guard
Instant Replay, 1968

DON SHINNICK—Colts 1957–1969

Don Shinnick . . . was a linebacker, of all things, and yet he had probably the strangest body in the history of the world.

Bill Curry, former center

LAWRENCE TAYLOR—Giants 1981–

He came on a blitz one time, and I was just trying to beat him to the handoff.

Eric Dickerson, Rams tailback

FREDD YOUNG—Seahawks and Colts 1984–

I would rather sandpaper a bobcat's butt in a phone booth than be tackled by Fredd.

Bryan Millard, Seahawks guard
The Oregonian, 1987

 MODERN DAYS/OLDEN DAYS

The game has passed into the hands of experts and veterans. No longer can it be considered a Saturday afternoon pastime for bank clerks to go out and rub the college boys in the mud.

Phil Weaver, Jr., writer
The Overland Monthly, 1893

Ballplayers are not made up of that old vigor. These days when Sunday rolls around, there's like to be too much kibitzing going on, which ought to be left in the bedroom.

Dick "Night Train" Lane,
Lions cornerback, 1963

The public today is ready to accept a new view of sports.
Grantland Rice described Notre Dame's backfield as the
Four Horsemen of the Apocalypse. Hell, today they look to
me like nothing more than four guys who are probably
flunking algebra.

> Jim Murray, sports columnist
> *Newsweek,* 1968

That gig is over now, and I blame it on Vince Lombardi.
The success of his Green Bay approach in the '60s restruc-
tured the game entirely. Lombardi never really thought
about *winning;* his trip was *not losing.*

> Hunter S. Thompson, writer
> *Rolling Stone,* 1974

Football players used to have names like Bulldog Turner
and Bronko Nagurski. Now they have names like Lynn
Swann. Can you believe that?

> Lonnie Shoor, comedian, 1981

By the time you learn all the handshakes, the season is
over.

> Johnny Unitas, Colts quarterback
> *Sports Illustrated,* 1981

We were too tired. We used to play offense and defense.

> Bronko Nagurski,
> former Bears running back,
> on high-five handshakes
> and dances in the end zones

In my day you were a sissy if you wore a facemask. Of
course, with my face it didn't matter.

> Art Donovan,
> former Colts defensive tackle
> "Late Night with David Letterman,"
> NBC-TV, 1983

What you have now is entertainment. What we had was real football.

> Joe Schmidt, former Lions linebacker

When I was a rookie and heard a sports car coming up, it was always a veteran. Now when I hear a sports car coming or see an expensive car in the lot, it's usually a rookie.

> Joe DeLamielleure, Browns guard
> *Chicago Sun-Times,* 1985

I'd have to have an agent, too, because I couldn't keep from laughing if I asked for that kind of money to play football.

> Red Grange, former running back
> *Sports Illustrated,* 1985

When I first started pro football, I was king of the weight room. Twelve years later they don't even consider me queen.

> Dennis Harrah,
> Rams offensive tackle
> *Inside Sports,* 1987

When I started in the NFL in 1950, the league ran on Johnson & Johnson tape and beer, not necessarily in that order. Without either, the league would have folded.

> Art Donovan,
> former Colts defensive tackle
> *Fatso,* 1987

"Would you like a cocktail?" they always ask. It used to be, "Would you like a *drink?*" You used to have a drink and eat spaghetti. Now you have a cocktail and eat pasta.

> John Madden, CBS-TV broadcaster
> *One Size Doesn't Fit All,* 1988

MONDAY NIGHT FOOTBALL

This is me, Howard Cosell, who just this afternoon had lunch with Chou En-lai, telling you that that pass was overthrown!!!

Larry Merchant, sportswriter
*And Every Day You Take
Another Bite*, 1971

Cosell: John, you gave us a good show.
Madden: Show! A great show! To you it's a show but to me it's a goddamn game we just lost!

John Madden, Raiders coach,
to Howard Cosell after a 21–20
loss to the Bills, 1974

I have tried terribly to like Howard, and I have failed miserably.

Red Smith, sportswriter
The New York Times

If Cosell were a sport, he would be roller derby.

Jimmy Cannon, columnist

Who else would have the courage to go up to Johnny Unitas and say, "All right, your name is Johnny Unitas, your arm is shot, you can't throw the bomb anymore, your career is over. How do you feel?" I mean, who else would *do* that?

Jim Bouton, sportswriter and former
baseball pitcher
Gallery, 1973

I'm disappointed Howard Cosell can't be here tonight, too. I keep forgetting Doak Walker's number.

Jim Murray, sports columnist,
at a roast, 1979

Later on, Howard Cosell will come out here and let us boo him before the football season starts.

> Johnny Carson
> "The Tonight Show," NBC-TV, 1981

Howard has stopped asking questions. He's too busy interviewing himself.

> Larry King, talk show host, 1985

Howard was the perfect sportscaster—he had two minutes of knowledge about everything.

> Gene Klein, former Chargers owner
> *First Down and a Billion*, 1987

He has no more business in the ABC press box for "Monday Night Football" than I do. When you take the game seriously you want information, not gibberish, and the smooth gray call of a professional football creature like Frank Gifford.

> Hunter S. Thompson, writer
> *Generation of Swine*, 1988

It's a traveling freak show.

> Don Meredith, "Monday Night
> Football" broadcaster
> *Los Angeles Times*, 1981

We're all guilty of it. We zoom in. . . . "Oh, isn't that awful. . . . Let's look at it again in slow motion. . . . Whoops, there goes his head." I'm told that . . . if the fans don't get to see those things, man, the switchboard lights up.

> Don Meredith

There's got to be more to life than what's going on down there.

> Don Meredith
> "Monday Night Football," ABC-TV

The word for Don is insouciant. He understands that the contests don't really mean a damn thing, and I respect that very much.

> Howard Cosell, "Monday Night
> Football" broadcaster
> *The Washington Post,* 1979

Don Meredith is nobody's fool. He is no more a country bumpkin than Howard Cosell is Jack the Ripper.

> Robert Friedman, sportswriter
> *Inside Sports,* 1980

The only trouble we had with Don Meredith was hoping he could find the right city.

> Frank Gifford, "Monday Night
> Football" broadcaster
> *The Sporting News,* 1986

Frank Gifford is the only sportscaster who adamantly and fiercely allows the event to speak for itself.

> Frederick Exley, writer
> *Inside Sports,* 1979

Where Cosell can deliver a compliment as if it were an insult, Gifford sounds nice even when he's trying to be tough.

> Robert Friedman, sportswriter
> *Inside Sports,* 1980

Gifford is about as colorful as cream cheese on white bread with mayo, and now that English is our official language, could be in a big trouble situation.

> Herb Caen, columnist
> *San Francisco Chronicle,* 1986

Monday night is a circus night—it's a week-long pep rally. It scares you to have to go on the road.

> Bud Grant, Vikings coach
> *Minneapolis Star*

That's Otis Sistrunk. He's from the University of Mars.

> Alex Karras, broadcaster, on the
> Raiders defensive lineman
> "Monday Night Football," ABC-TV

He's just telling us, "They're number 1."

> Don Meredith, after a fan made an
> obscene hand gesture
> "Monday Night Football," ABC-TV

Al [Michaels] is inquisitive, knowledgeable, and incredibly well prepared. I don't know what his IQ is, but it's probably only a couple of points lower than mine.

> Dan Dierdorf, Michaels's partner on
> "Monday Night Football"
> *Sports Illustrated*, 1987

 **MONEY**

I'll tell you what, kid. You should think about playing up in Canada. It's a lovely country, you know. There's only one problem. The snow is up to your ass in June.

> Nick Kerbawy, Lions general
> manager, when defensive tackle Alex
> Karras asked for $12,000 as a rookie,
> 1962

There's no principle involved in my holdout. Only money.

> O. J. Simpson, Bills unsigned rookie
> *Sports Illustrated*, 1969

If O.J.'s asking for $600,000, maybe it will take a $600,000 man to stop him.

> Joe Greene, Steelers unsigned rookie
> defensive tackle, 1969

Anybody who says they're not in it for the money is full of shit.

> Fred Biletnikoff, Raiders receiver

Jimmy [Taylor] was a very tough negotiator on contracts, but [Vince] Lombardi was, too. Sometimes he would just tell a guy, "You get your ass up there and sign that contract." And they'd do it.

> Bill Curry, former Packers center
> *One More July,* 1977

Making money has never been a big problem. Keeping it has sometimes been a different ball game.

> Ken Stabler, Oilers quarterback
> *Inside Sports,* 1980

I'm bored, I'm broke, and I'm back.

> John Riggins, Redskins running
> back, after a one-year layoff, 1981

When I was a kid, our land was so poor we had to fertilize the house just to raise the windows.

> Bum Phillips, Saints coach
> *Playboy,* 1981

Right after he grabbed me by the ankles and dangled me out of an eleventh-floor window.

> Gil Brandt, Cowboys personnel
> executive, on when he reached
> agreement with linebacker
> Randy White, 1981

My opening argument was that Cliff kept the dry-cleaning bill down on his uniform.

> Richard Glazer, agent for backup
> Steelers quarterback Cliff Stoudt
> *The Sporting News,* 1981

I fired my first agent because he was incompetent. His name was Bruce Harper.

> Bruce Harper, Jets receiver
> *Sports Illustrated,* 1983

A couple of days after I signed, a guy called my stepfather asking for a $130,000 loan. He said he needed the money because he had a cure for cancer, AIDS, and leukemia.

> Eric Dickerson, Rams running back,
> on becoming a millionaire
> *The Sporting News,* 1983

We don't supply women, so it must be money.

> Bum Phillips, Saints coach, when
> asked if linebacker Dennis Winston's
> holdout was over money
> *Los Angeles Times,* 1985

High finance to me is enough dough for a hunk of kosher salami, a loaf of Jewish rye, and a case of Schlitz.

> Art Donovan,
> former Colts defensive tackle
> *Fatso,* 1987

I was scared. I thought Detroit was going to draft me. I was going to ask for so much money that they'd have had to put me on layaway.

> Deion Sanders, Falcons defensive
> back
> "Gameday," ESPN-TV, 1989

NFL TEAMS

ATLANTA FALCONS

I think last year we believed we were better than we really were. I think we're better than we were then. But we can't think we're better than we really are.

> Leeman Bennett, Falcons coach,
> 1981. (In 1980, Atlanta was 12–4;
> they finished 7–9 in 1981.)

The status of local sports may be best summed up by a popular bumper sticker . . . GO BRAVES—AND TAKE THE FALCONS WITH YOU.

Peter Applebome, writer
The New York Times, 1989

BUFFALO BILLS

We drink enough every Saturday night to convince us the Bills have a chance to win. By the time we sober up, it's the third quarter and it's too late to leave. So we watch 'em lose again.

Doug Graham, Bills fan
USA Today, 1984

The continued progress of quarterback Jim Kelly leaves the Bills, according to club sources, only forty-four players shy of a good team.

Mike Downey, sports columnist
The Sporting News, 1986

CHICAGO BEARS

The Bears hang out in Chicago bars you wouldn't advise your worst enemy to go to.

Alex Karras, Lions defensive tackle,
early 1960s

Mirro Roder is going to be the best field goal kicker in our league in a year or two. Well, so much for our offense.

Dick Butkus, Bears linebacker, 1973.
(Roder played two years
with the Bears.)

We don't want it, America's Team. That's too syrupy. Now if you want to call us America's Degenerate Team, that's different.

Keith Van Horne,
Bears offensive tackle
The Sporting News, 1985

This team is just goofy enough to win it all again.

> Bob Verdi, sportswriter
> *The Sporting News*, 1986

CINCINNATI BENGALS

When do the batteries run out on those?

> Dan Hampton, Bears defensive end,
> when the Bengals introduced their
> striped helmets, 1981

The team looks like it's just been run over by a Goodyear radial.

> Ron Martz, sportswriter,
> on the new uniforms
> *Atlanta Journal*, 1981

Okay, listen, you guys. I know you got problems there. You got steel mills shutting down. You got highways with holes in 'em. You got Akron. You got the Cleveland Indians *and* the Cincinnati Bengals.

> "Joe Bob Briggs," a.k.a. John Bloom,
> columnist
> *Dallas Times-Herald*, 1984

Doesn't it seem, uh, like there should be two *n*'s in Cincinnati? I mean a double *n* in the middle. Isn't that odd? You live here for years and you still aren't sure.

> Sam Wyche, Bengals coach
> *Sports Illustrated*, 1989

CLEVELAND BROWNS

Instead of looking around the front office for a scapegoat, the fans should look around the bars where the players were enjoying their 1980 prestige.

> Brian Sipe, Browns quarterback
> *Sports Illustrated*, 1982

No other player in any sport here has said he dreamed of playing in Cleveland.

> Art Modell, Browns owner, praising
> quarterback Bernie Kosar
> *Sports Illustrated,* 1985

Will the next person that sees *anybody* throw *anything* on this field point him out—we'll get him out of here. You don't live in Cleveland, you live in Cincinnati!

> Sam Wyche, Bengals coach, on
> the public address system, to
> fans throwing snowballs on the
> field, 1989

DALLAS COWBOYS

George never used to say "the Dallas Cowboys." It was always "the goddamned Dallas Cowboys."

> John Wilbur, former Cowboys and
> Redskins lineman, on Redskins coach
> George Allen

What kind of place has a domed stadium with a hole in the roof that's only over the field? . . . The first time I ever played there, it was raining. I turned to Ben Davidson and said, "Do you know what's happening here?" He said, "Yeah, it's raining." I said, "But only on the players, Ben, only on us."

> Tom Keating, former Raiders
> defensive lineman
> *Sports Illustrated,* 1982

Texas Stadium has a hole in its roof so God can watch his favorite team play.

> D. D. Lewis,
> former Cowboys linebacker
> *The Sporting News,* 1982

We're the second most [hated team]. We'll never catch Dallas.

Al Davis,
Raiders managing general partner
Sports Illustrated, 1982

Sagebrush, U.S.A. Their fans don't know football, they just know something's wrong if the Cowboys aren't winning by two TDs.

Tom Brookshier, CBS-TV broadcaster
Sports Illustrated, 1982

They never give anyone credit. Whenever someone beats them, all you hear is, "Well, those weren't the real Dallas Cowboys they beat." How many guys do they carry on their roster, anyway?

John Brodie, NBC-TV broadcaster,
1982

Talk to anyone around the league and they'll tell you, "We don't care who wins, as long as it isn't the Cowboys."

Jack Lambert, Steelers linebacker,
1982

The Cowboys are like a woman who's had a lot of facelifts. They're a fantasy from their uniforms to their stadium, which is like being in a living room. They have this holier-than-thou attitude that makes me sick.

Howie Long, Raiders defensive end
Gentlemen's Quarterly, 1984

"I hate the Cowboys," Priscilla said. "Talk about stuck-up people."

Dan Jenkins,
sportswriter and novelist
Life Its Ownself, 1984

Even if you've only *tried out* for the Cowboys, you're a hero.

Harvey Martin, former Cowboys
defensive end
Texas Thunder, 1986

DENVER BRONCOS

Who's the last Bronco quarterback to be selected for the Pro Bowl? The answer is nobody. Denver quarterbacks have been the guys to hold 'em until the defense can get back on the field and force a turnover.

> Paul Zimmerman, football analyst
> *Sports Illustrated*, 1986

Our curfew is very simple. We only have a one-man team, so we just have to make sure number 7 (quarterback John Elway) makes the curfew. The other forty-four guys can do whatever they want.

> Dan Reeves, Broncos coach, 1988

DETROIT LIONS

One thing about that team. We had 100 percent attendance at all parties.

> Bobby Layne, former Lions
> quarterback, on the mid-1950s

You can dress up Pontiac, but you can't take it out of Detroit.

> Skip Bayless, sports columnist
> *Dallas Morning News*, 1982

The Lions continue to fool the experts by making most of their defeats close.

> Mike Downey, sports columnist
> *The Sporting News*, 1986

GREEN BAY PACKERS

The Packers were the most soft-bitten team in the league. They overwhelmed one opponent, underwhelmed ten, and whelmed one.

> Red Smith, sportswriter, on
> the 1–10–1 record the year before
> Vince Lombardi took over in 1959

You will drop passes. You will make mistakes. But not very many if you want to play for the Green Bay Packers.

Vince Lombardi, Packers coach, 1967

Can you imagine what it would be like playing all season in Green Bay? No thanks. If I had to play someplace like that, I believe I would get out and go to work for a living.

Craig Morton, Cowboys quarterback, 1972

Last place in Green Bay is the coldest place on earth.

Gary Smith, sportswriter
Inside Sports, 1980

Martina Navratilova is like the old Green Bay Packers. You know exactly what she's going to do, but there isn't a thing you can do about it.

Arthur Ashe, tennis player, on
Lombardi's teams
The Sporting News, 1983

If there was a contest and there were ninety-seven prizes, the ninety-eighth would be a trip to Green Bay.

John McKay, Buccaneers coach
USA Today, 1984

I like the color of our uniform.

Forrest Gregg, Packers coach, asked
what he liked about the Packers,
1986

When people in Green Bay say they have a nice wardrobe it means they have ten bowling shirts.

Greg Koch, Dolphins offensive tackle
Sports Illustrated, 1986

I'm happy to be a Packer. I did call Green Bay a "village" in *Playboy,* but every village needs a village idiot.

Tony Mandarich, Packers guard,
1989

HOUSTON OILERS

The problem for us is the game always starts an hour early.

> Bum Phillips, Oilers coach, on their
> inability to score early
> "Thursday Night Edition," ABC-TV,
> 1980

If the Oilers offense were a horse, it would be a Clydesdale. Earl Campbell off tackle, Earl Campbell on a slant, incomplete ten-yard square out, punt, flash the sign that says "DeeeFense."

> Glen Waggoner, sportswriter
> *Sport,* 1982

In Minnesota I look up at the scoreboard to see the score. In Houston I looked up to see how much time was left.

> Dave Casper, Vikings tight end,
> from Houston
> *Sports Illustrated,* 1983

If it's the eighth wonder of the world, the rent is the ninth.

> Bud Adams, Oilers owner,
> on the Astrodome
> *Sports Ilustrated,* 1984

INDIANAPOLIS/BALTIMORE COLTS

I looked at the bodies on the Colts team and wondered if we'd ever win a game. It was like wandering into the locker room of the YMCA.

> Bill Curry, center, coming from the
> Packers to the Colts in 1967

We're called the Colts--horses. They've got that right. We've got a lot of old nags around here.

> Frank Kush, arriving to take over the
> Colts, 2–14 the previous year, 1982

Do you know how the Colts got their name? Because Maryland is famous as thoroughbred country? Now what does Colts have to do with Indianapolis?

> John Steadman, former Colts
> assistant general manager
> *The New York Times,* 1984

I think he's crazy. If they're going to take the Colts out of Baltimore, there should be no more Colts. Call them the Indianapolis Air Conditioners. That's how he made his money.

> Ray Perkins, former Colts receiver,
> on owner Robert Irsay
> *The Sporting News,* 1984

The Colts do not need to draft Miami quarterback Vinny Testaverde—they need to draft *Miami.*

> Mike Downey, sports columnist
> *The Sporting News,* 1986

KANSAS CITY CHIEFS

I led the league in boos there.

> John Madden, former Raiders coach
> "The Tonight Show," NBC-TV, 1979

LOS ANGELES/OAKLAND RAIDERS

Dealing with the combined treacheries of the NFL and the Oakland Raiders is like trying to cover the National Swineherds Convention with a head full of PCP or spending ninety days as an outpatient at Folsom Prison.

> Hunter S. Thompson, writer
> *Rolling Stone,* 1974

Everywhere I've been, I've been the screwball on the team—in college, with the Colts, with the Packers—but here I'm just a normal guy.

> Ted Hendricks, Raiders linebacker,
> 1975

We're the Halfway House of the NFL.

> Gene Upshaw, Raiders guard
> *Sports Illustrated,* 1981

How many national commercials have you seen by a Raider? One—Ken Stabler throwing a can of oil. That will change in L.A.

> John Matuszak,
> Raiders defensive end
> *Sport,* 1982

Most of us are hesitant about declaring an allegiance to Al Davis and his warriors in silver and black. It's sort of, well, like embracing the plague or opting for communism.

> Loel Schrader
> *Long Beach Press-Telegram,* 1983

They're still the "Oakland" Raiders to me. The Raiders and Los Angeles don't go together. Los Angeles and Beverly Hills are Pacific Palisades and the Rolls-Royce and the glossy set. The Raiders go with the waterfront.

> Furman Bisher, sports columnist
> *The Sporting News,* 1984

Because of us there's the no-clothesline rule, the no-spearing rule, the no-hitting-out-of-bounds rule, the no-fumbling-forward-in-the-last-two-minutes-of-the-game rule, the no-throwing-helmets rule, and the no-Stickum rule. So you see, we're not all bad.

> Ted Hendricks, Raiders linebacker
> *Sports Illustrated,* 1984

The silver and black used to leave opponents black and blue. Their positions on defense were tackle, linebacker, cornerback, and armed robber. Not only were their bites worse than their barks, they could kill with their breath.

> Mike Downey, sports columnist
> *The Sporting News,* 1986

A lot of the Raiders are well-balanced players—they have a chip on *each* shoulder.

> Don Criqui, sportscaster
> "NFL Football," NBC-TV, 1986

Given their reputation, when you look down the Raiders roster for the institutions of higher learning they have come from, you have to expect to see alma maters like the University of Just Win, Baby, the I'm Innocent I Tell You Correctional Institution, Electric Chair Tech, and Up the River State College.

> Jim Murray, sports columnist
> *Los Angeles Times*, 1986

The Oakland Raiders used to have half jerseys, slobbering, spitting, scratching, fighting. That was silver-and-black football. . . . This team is definitely going L.A. now.

> Lester Hayes, Raiders cornerback
> *Sports Illustrated*, 1987

LOS ANGELES RAMS

We live in a strange state over here. We have earthquakes, fires, floods, the Los Angeles Rams.

> Johnny Carson
> "The Tonight Show," NBC-TV, 1979

I'm a shot-and-beer guy, and that was a martini town.

> Ron Jaworski,
> former Rams quarterback
> *Sports Illustrated*, 1981

To think that I went out and slaved in the trenches all those Sundays to send my kids through school, getting my thumbs bent back so that I went like this in pain, "AIEEE!" while all the time the kids were rooting for these guys across the line because they had nice-looking logos on their helmets designed by some interior decorator in Pasadena.

> Alex Karras, former Lions defensive
> tackle, on the Rams helmets
> *Sports Illustrated*, 1981

Los Angeles fans never stay till the end of the game. It's part of the local culture. People in Los Angeles even leave sex early to beat the traffic.

Scott Ostler, sports columnist
Los Angeles Times, 1982

There's no better training ground for criticism than playing quarterback for the Los Angeles Rams.

Pat Haden, former Rams
quarterback, now CBS-TV
commentator, 1982

Waiting for the Rams to win a Super Bowl is like leaving the porch light on for Jimmy Hoffa.

Milton Berle, comedian, 1984

With seven interceptions in his last two games, [Dan] Marino's skills have deteriorated to such an extent that the Rams are now considering making an offer for him.

Steve Harvey, syndicated columnist,
1986

MIAMI DOLPHINS

How can I root for a team that's the name of a fish?

Avery Corman, novelist
The Old Neighborhood, 1980

I've already inquired, and we would be favored over Miami by anywhere from seven to ten points.

Paul Hornung, former Packers
running back, when asked how his
teams would do against the great
Miami teams

MINNESOTA VIKINGS

This isn't a disco town. It's a polka town.

Bud Grant, Vikings coach, 1982

It's hard to pick out our stars. It would have to be an aw-fully dark night to find them.

> Bud Grant
> *Sports Illustrated*, 1985

That surface also happens to be exceptionally safe for fans in the upper decks. If they fall out of the stands, they have a good chance of bouncing right back up to their seats.

> Ron Luciano, former baseball umpire
> on the Metrodome's artificial turf
> *The Fall of the Roman Umpire*, 1986

NEW ENGLAND PATRIOTS

This team will never win. I am worried about their chart: This team's destiny is to be star-crossed because they'll come close to winning but never do it.

> Michael Madden, quoting on *Boston Globe*
> astrologer, on the team's 1959 birthdate,
> 1981. (The Patriots won the AFC
> Championship in 1985 but suffered the
> then biggest defeat in Super Bowl history,
> 46–10, at the hands of the Bears.)

NEW ORLEANS SAINTS

"A veteran on the Saints is someone who has been here through at least six coaches," said one player who has yet to qualify.

> John Papanek, sportswriter
> *Sports Illustrated*, 1981

Better not take too long, or someone else will be teaching them.

> Bum Phillips, Saints coach,
> when asked how long his rebuilding
> would take, 1981

The Saints need help everywhere but at the hot-dog stand.

> Anson Mount, football analyst
> *Playboy*, 1982

The Saints are a terrible team, coached by Bum Phillips, who has as much imagination as an avocado.

> Lowell Cohn, sports columnist
> *San Francisco Chronicle*, 1985

New Orleans is a darn nice place to hold a Super Bowl. For one thing, you never have to worry about having a neutral site. The day the Saints make the Super Bowl is the day Bum Phillips costars in a movie with Meryl Streep.

> Mike Downey, sports columnist
> *The Sporting News*, 1986

NEW YORK GIANTS

We had three-hundred-pound linemen who couldn't cross an intersection at a dead run and beat the light.

> Fran Tarkenton, former Giants
> quarterback, on the 1967 team
> *Broken Patterns*, 1971

The self-image of the perfect Giant was a cool, well-mannered gentleman with close-cropped hair and a Brooks Brothers suit whose briefcase was packed with football plays and bond quotations. Horn-rimmed glasses were optional.

> Fran Tarkenton, on the 1968 team
> *Broken Patterns*, 1971

You want to know about the typical Giants fan? He gets excited every year and says, "We're goin' to the Super Bowl." Then when the team goes in the tank, he starts rememberin' the old days. He starts in with Huff and Robustelli and Y. A. Tittle. The true Giants fan doesn't remember that they gotta play Dallas twice every year.

> John Madden, CBS-TV broadcaster
> *Boston Globe*, 1983

It's autumn here in New York City, and the crisp, cool air is heavy with the smoky aroma of Giants fans burning their season tickets.

> David Letterman
> "Late Night with David Letterman,"
> NBC-TV, 1985

NEW YORK JETS

Loyal Jets fans were easy to recognize in my day. You just looked for the little old lady being mugged, and there they were.

> Dan Jenkins, sportswriter and novelist
> *Life Its Ownself,* 1984

The New York Jets should trade their play-off spot to the Seattle Seahawks for an offense to be named later.

> Dave Anderson, sports columnist
> *The New York Times,* 1986

PHILADELPHIA EAGLES

Our offensive line is so good our own backs can't even get through it.

> Billy Barnes, Eagles running back,
> c. 1960

How bad are the Eagles? They are worse than inept. They are even worse than un-ept. They are so far away from ept, it's a toll call.

> Tony Kornheiser, sportswriter
> *The Washington Post,* 1984

The Eagles fans, perhaps the finest booers in the NFL.

> Paul Zimmerman, football analyst
> *The New Thinking Man's Guide to*
> *Pro Football,* 1984

You know how you can tell a *real* Eagles fan? It's someone who leaves the game and says *what* cheerleaders?

> Tim Reid, comedian
> "Thanksgiving Parade," CBS-TV,
> 1984

They ought to call Buddy Ryan's defense 35 instead of 46 because the opponents average thirty-five points a game.

> Arne Harris, producer/director
> "Cubs Baseball," WGN-TV, Chicago,
> 1986

Fans here don't boo just anybody. They boo the best.

> Ralph Wiley, sportswriter
> *Sports Illustrated*, 1989

PHOENIX/ST. LOUIS CARDINALS

Is St. Louis the national headquarters for McDonald's?

> D. D. Lewis, Cowboys rookie
> linebacker, on first seeing the
> Gateway Arch, 1968

It could give you some extra pay, and you've got a good chance of not getting hit.

> Jim Hanifan, Cardinals coach,
> offering sportswriters the chance to
> be tackling dummies, 1983

Our defense was horrible. In fact, it was so bad, when the opposing offense had a third and ten, we didn't even bother to stand and stretch.

> Conrad Dobler, Cardinals guard in
> the mid-1970s
> *They Call Me Dirty*, 1988

PITTSBURGH STEELERS

The biggest thrill wasn't winning on Sunday but meeting the payroll on Monday.

> Art Rooney, Steelers owner, on the
> early days of the franchise, 1978

You know, I'm a defensive tackle, too, but I'm afraid of these guys.

> Tom Keating, coming from the
> Raiders to join Ernie Holmes, "Mean
> Joe" Greene, L. C. Greenwood, and
> Dwight White, 1973

I do remember you had to play the Steelers with your helmet screwed on tight.

> Gene Upshaw, Raiders guard
> *San Jose Mercury News*, 1980

Pittsburgh Steelers fans lead the league in collective lunacy. Their elevators don't stop at the top floor

> Tim McCarver, sportscaster
> "Not So Great Moments in Sports,"
> HBO-TV, 1986

SAN DIEGO CHARGERS

The way the Chargers played, the drug must have been formaldehyde.

> Bill Kurtis, broadcaster,
> on drug abuse allegations
> among the 1974 Chargers

If they want scoring, why don't we just let the Chargers play every Monday night? Nobody can stop them from scoring, and they can't stop anybody.

> Art Modell, Browns owner, 1978

Question: What can fly like an eagle but sooner or later turns into a pigeon?
Answer: The San Diego Chargers.

> Phil Musick, sports columnist
> *USA Today*, 1983

Tell owner Gene Klein I'll pay him $35 million for them and he can keep the defense.

> Gary McCord, golf broadcaster, upon
> hearing the Chargers were for sale
> for $70 million
> "Panasonic Las Vegas Invitational,"
> ESPN-TV, 1984

A new coach is attempting to convince the Chargers that it is okay to keep trying, even when the other team has the ball.

> Mike Downey, sports columnist
> *The Sporting News*, 1986

The Chargers, it became apparent, were the sporting world's version of a used car—shiny on the outside but just good enough on the inside to make it through the warranty period.

> Gene Klein, former Chargers owner,
> on the late 1960s
> *First Down and a Billion*, 1987

San Diego is blessed with the finest climate in the United States. If someone throws a candy wrapper on the ground in San Diego, a candy tree will sprout.

> Gene Klein
> *First Down and a Billion*, 1987

SAN FRANCISCO 49ERS

The fans in this area were starved for success—and we'd usually been the ones withholding the food.

> Randy Cross, 49ers guard
> *San Francisco Chronicle*, 1982

Hopefully, our white wine-sipping crowd will decide to get off its collective ass and cheer.

> Randy Cross, before a big game
> *San Francisco Examiner*, 1986

SEATTLE SEAHAWKS

I love the town and the people, but I don't understand why everybody is trying to push salmon on me. I hate salmon.

> Franco Harris,
> Seahawks running back
> *Seattle Post-Intelligencer*, 1984

If you want to know what it's like, put a pot on your head
and beat on it with a spoon.

> Randy Cross, 49ers guard, on the
> Kingdome noise
> *USA Today,* 1985

When the best play your quarterback makes all night is a
tackle, it's just about time to pack your football away with
your other toys and forget about the Super Bowl for another
year.

> Gordon Edes, sports columnist
> *Los Angeles Times,* 1985

Dressed predominantly in Seahawk blue and gray, carrying
football paraphernalia, and hooting and hollering, the fans
look like invaders come to wipe out downtown civilization.

> Fred Moody, sportswriter
> *Fighting Chance,* 1989

TAMPA BAY BUCCANEERS

My humor was appreciated in California, but it goes over
the heads of people in Florida.

> John McKay, Buccaneers coach
> *The Sporting News,* 1983

Overlooked in all the excitement was the announcement by
Tampa Bay (2–12) that, effective at the end of this season,
it was dropping its football program.

> Steve Harvey, syndicated columnist,
> 1986

Tampa is sunsets that make you cry and a professional football team that breaks your heart.

> Jack Whittaker, sports broadcaster
> "J. C. Penney Classic," ABC-TV,
> 1986

WASHINGTON REDSKINS

The Redskins are the only thing in Washington that the people think of as "ours." Nobody in Washington gives a tinker's damn about the Kennedy Center or the Washington Symphony.

Richard M. Nixon, 1979

A loss by the Redskins can affect the way the government works on Mondays. Federal employees will take it out on the social security program, various federal grant programs, military spending, and the policies of the state department. They are that depressed. So it is definitely in the national interest for the rest of the NFL to let Washington's Redskins win.

Art Buchwald, humorist, 1982

 **OFFENSIVE LINEMEN**

When Tiny put the shot, the shot stayed put.

Bugs Baer, humorist, on University of Chicago guard Tiny Maxwell, 1902

No wonder centers get confused. They're always looking at the world upside down and backwards.

Bob Zuppke, Illinois coach

I'm an offensive lineman. I don't get a lot of publicity and don't ask for any. All I get out of it is an immense satisfaction. Football is rules and discipline, and I happen to think that's what life is all about.

David Browning, Texas Tech
offensive tackle
Sports Illustrated, 1971

There's this interior lineman. He's as big as a gorilla and strong as a gorilla. Now, if he was as smart as a gorilla, we'd be fine.

Sam Bailey,
University of Tampa coach
Sports Illustrated, 1972

Guard that gap the way a mother guards her virgin daughter.

Joe Madro,
Packers offensive line coach

Let's face it. The reason you're playing offense is because you ain't good enough to play defense. When you play guard, it's because you aren't smart enough to be quarterback, not fast enough to be a halfback, not rugged enough to be a fullback, not big enough to be a tackle, and don't have the hands of an end.

Dick Bestwick,
Georgia offensive line coach

If the meek are going to inherit the earth, our offensive linemen are going to be land barons.

Bill Muir, Southern Methodist
offensive line coach

I've gone months without ever touching the ball in a game. And if you ever do touch it, it's because somebody screwed up.

Tom Glassic, Broncos guard
San Francisco Chronicle, 1981

I've compared offensive linemen to the story of Paul Revere. After Paul Revere rode through town, everybody said what a great job he did. But no one ever talked about the horse.

Gene Upshaw, Raiders guard

As an old center, I know what it's like to be number 2.

Gerald R. Ford, former Michigan
center, 1974

There's nothing wrong with him except he played football too long—without a helmet

> Lyndon B. Johnson, on Ford

How come you always get the nice, dedicated head butters, and I get all the loonies and whackos, like Coy Bacon and now the new one the 'Skins have, the guy with the arrow on his head, Dexter Manley? It's not fair.

> Stan Walters, to fellow Eagles
> offensive tackle Jerry Sizemore, 1981

He's so short his breath smells of earthworms.

> Ron Meyer, Southern Methodist
> coach, on five-foot-nine guard
> Harvey McAtee
> *Sports Illustrated*, 1981

I understand women better than linemen. I simply can't figure out why anybody would want to play a position where you get beat all around and you don't even touch the ball.

> Ahmad Rashad, Vikings receiver
> *Sports Illustrated*, 1982

The key is holding your blocks. The offensive line coach always says, "Keep your space and stay off your face."

> Frank Broyles, former coach
> "Gator Bowl," ABC-TV, 1983

It's better to die at birth than jump offside at the goal line.

> Tom Freeman, Arizona State
> offensive line coach
> *Seattle Post-Intelligencer*, 1984

A defensive lineman comes up to the coach, spits on the floor, doesn't bother to comb his hair, and says, "How much are you going to pay me to play for you?" An offensive lineman is a nice guy who has his hair neatly combed and mildly inquires, "Where would you prefer that I play?"

Buddy Ryan,
Bears defensive coordinator
USA Today, 1984

People have never yet paid to see a great blocker.

Paul Zimmerman, football analyst
*The New Thinking Man's Guide to
Pro Football,* 1984

You can't have timid people on the offensive line when there are crazies on the defensive line. You've got to be just as nuts. Our guys are. They're a bunch of sick puppies.

Jim McMahon, Bears quarterback
The Sporting News, 1985

As you keep growing up, only good enough to play offensive line, you try to do it the best you can and pretty soon you excel at that and you keep on progressing. But all you ever progress to be is an offensive lineman.

Dennis Harrah, Rams guard
Inside Sports, 1987

All those quarterbacks feel the same to me.

Jay Hilgenberg, Bears center
Sports Illustrated, 1987

I'm the only offensive lineman in the history of football who was called for holding, tripping, and clipping *before* the snap.

Conrad Dobler, former guard
They Call Me Dirty, 1988

They all sit on the same end of the bench during games, and they always sit in the same order.

Connie Millard, wife of Seahawks
offensive tackle Bryan Millard, 1988

I always wondered about those trenches. Where is the trench everybody talks about?

Paul Maguire, NBC-TV analyst, 1988

It takes a Pro Bowl player to move me out of my position. Unfortunately, they keep finding them.

David Huffman,
Vikings guard and tackle
San Francisco Chronicle, 1990

DICK AFFLIS—PACKERS 1951–1964

Afflis got married and divorced so many times, he couldn't remember which wife got what in alimony payments.

Alex Karras
Even Big Guys Cry, 1977

BILL BAIN—PACKERS, BRONCOS, GIANTS, RAMS, JETS, AND PATRIOTS 1975–1986

Once, when an official dropped a flag and penalized the Rams for having twelve men on the field, . . . two of them were Bain.

Jim Murray, sports columnist
Los Angeles Times

CHARLEY COWAN—RAMS 1961–1975

His idea of pass blocking is a crunching bear hug followed by a knee to the groin and a forearm to the chin.

Pat Toomay, former defensive end
The Crunch, 1975

DOUG DIEKEN—BROWNS 1971–1984

He always has something to say. He's always calling for a draw play to make his job easier.

Paul McDonald, Browns quarterback
San Francisco Examiner, 1983

CONRAD DOBLER—CARDINALS, SAINTS, AND BILLS 1972–1982

He is holding. Now, folks, you'll notice that he is tripping.
There you have it, folks. Holding, tripping, kicking. All on
the *same* play. That's Conrad Dobler, folks, the dirtiest
player in professional football.

> Alex Karras, analyst
> "Monday Night Football," ABC-TV,
> 1975

I'm sure someone will break his neck along the line, and I
won't send flowers.

> Merlin Olsen, Rams tackle, 1975

To say Dobler "plays" football is like saying the Gestapo
"played" Twenty Questions. It's like being in a pup tent
with a grizzly.

> Jim Murray, sports columnist
> *Los Angeles Times*

Playing against Dobler, they say, is like grabbing onto the
wrong end of a chainsaw.

> Ray Didinger, sportswriter
> *Philadelphia Bulletin*

JOHN HANNAH—PATRIOTS 1973–1982

Once we measured John's thighs, and they were thirty-three
inches. I said, "I can't bear it. They're bigger than my bust."

> Page Hannah, wife of John
> *Sports Illustrated*, 1981

MEL HEIN—GIANTS 1931–1945

Mel Hein, the Hall of Fame center, . . . was in a crouch so
long I think it took him fifteen years to see the sun.

> John McKay,
> Southern California coach
> *McKay: A Coach's Story*, 1975

BOB HYLAND—Packers, Giants, Patriots, and Bears 1967–1977

Look at that stance, Hyland. What can you do from that stance? You can't do anything. You can't go right. You can't go left. You can't block. The only thing that stance is good for is taking a crap.

> Vince Lombardi, Packers coach, 1967

HENRY LAWRENCE—Raiders 1974–1986

It's like standing in the middle of a freeway.

> Ken Stabler,
> former Raiders quarterback,
> on Lawrence's pass blocking
> *San Jose Mercury News*, 1981

JIM PARKER—Colts 1957–1967

I worked two years on a single move against Parker, and it fooled him just once.

> Henry Jordan,
> Packers defensive tackle, 1973

We could tell how much he weighed by the wrinkles in his neck. If he had three wrinkles, he weighed 290. Four and he weighed 310.

> Art Donovan,
> former Colts defensive tackle
> *USA Today*, 1984

HENRY SCHUH—Raiders and Packers 1965–1974

He was 280—and that reluctantly. Before he went to bed he would finish off a whole pizza by himself, then wash it down with a Diet Pepsi to show he was trying to lose weight.

> John Madden, CBS-TV broadcaster
> *Hey, Wait a Minute,*
> *I Wrote a Book!*, 1984

ART SHELL—RAIDERS 1968–1982

People always ask me what it's like to play against Art Shell, but the only way I can describe it is to ask them: "Have you ever been attacked by wild dogs?"

Lyle Alzado, Broncos defensive
lineman
Mile High, 1978

GENE UPSHAW—RAIDERS 1967–1982

Always up, always happy. If you were down and you talked to him, you soon were up. The way Gene is, if he were a dog, his tail would always be wagging.

John Madden, CBS-TV broadcaster
*Hey, Wait a Minute, I Wrote a
Book!*, 1984

CHRIS WARD—JETS, SAINTS, AND DOLPHINS 1978–1983

He married Jim Brown's daughter. The scouts are waiting for the offspring of that matchup.

Dick Enberg, sportscaster
The Sporting News, 1983

BOB YOUNG—CARDINALS, BRONCOS, OILERS, AND SAINTS 1966–1981

For his salad you just pour vinegar and oil on your lawn and let him graze.

Jim Bakken, former placekicker
Sports Illustrated, 1981

 ON THE ROAD

Did you know that the air is different in each town? And that the ball acts different in it? That's not so surprising. The water is slower here than in Tokyo. Did you know that?

> Gail Cogdill, Lions receiver, 1963

When you travel with the team and you eat with the team, you eat what the team eats.

> Vince Lombardi, Packers coach,
> when wife Marie wanted ice cream
> with her apple pie, 1966

Boy, this here place would sure hold a lot of hay.

> Tommy Joe Crutcher, Packers
> linebacker, formerly of Texas
> Christian, on Yankee Stadium, 1967

We worked out in Green Bay, flew to Baltimore, checked into our hotel, played poker for a couple of hours, ate an early dinner at the Chesapeake House, went back to the hotel, watched television, and went to sleep. It certainly is exciting to be a professional football player.

> Jerry Kramer, Packers guard
> *Instant Replay*, 1968

Nothing can be worse than this—lying around in a little hotel like a bunch of cruds. Then we get out on some field and knock some guys around for a lousy pile of pennies.

> Alex Karras, Lions defensive tackle

You'd be surprised how many girls there are who like to talk football in my hotel room.

> Joe Namath, Jets quarterback
> *I Can't Wait Until Tomorrow . . . ,*
> 1969

Where I come from, you go in a bar, you get in a fight, you prop the guy up, buy him a beer, you put your arm around him, and you're buddies. And if you break something, you pay the bartender. Out here, if you get in a fight, some silly bastard sues you.

> Marv Hubbard, Raiders fullback from
> Salamanca, New York, on a fracas
> near training camp in
> Santa Rosa, California

If you can't get it by eleven, you probably aren't going to get it anyway.

> George Blanda, Raiders quarterback,
> on road pursuits

I play as well on the road as I do at home. But my teams don't.

> Lou Holtz, Arkansas coach, 1981

That game wasn't a fair test. Not when the Humane Society is announcing that people should bring in their dogs for fear they'll freeze to death.

> Kellen Winslow, Chargers receiver,
> on playing in Cincinnati
> *San Jose Mercury News*, 1982

The stewardess asked if I'd like a bottle of wine. I asked, "French or American?" She said, "Neither. California."

> Charlie Jones, sportscaster,
> on a flight
> *The Sporting News*, 1984

The good Lord might not want to take me, but He might be after the pilot.

> Bobby Bowden, Florida State coach
> *The Sporting News*, 1984

OWNERS AND EXECUTIVES

A lot of the more evil problems of pro football might be cured if the owners were forced to cover one kickoff—and to repeat until they made one tackle, however long that took.

> Bernie Parrish, former defensive back
> *They Call It a Game*, 1971

I expected to walk in and see organized chaos. There was nothing organized about it.

> Harland Svare, Chargers general
> manager, on attending his first
> owners' meeting

I've given my children a great many things, but I've kept the football team for myself.

> Carroll Rosenbloom, Rams owner,
> 1978

I've always ducked out of sight when the coaches had to cut somebody. Then I'd write the guy and tell him how sorry I was.

> Art Rooney, Steelers owner
> *Inside Sports*, 1981

I work for John Mecom, and I know that sumbitch likes me. That's a far sight better than working for some sumbitch that don't like me.

> Bum Phillips, Saints coach,
> on the team's owner
> *Sport*, 1983

If I'd wanted a seat in the stands, I could have bought one for $12.

> John Mecom, Saints owner, on why
> he sat in a private box

Damned if I know. I think it's in lieu of a raise.

John McKay, Buccaneers coach,
given the title of vice president
Sport, 1983

[Owners are] all in the grueling business of tax avoidance. They all want somebody to give them a modern facility that holds eighty thousand people and a wine cellar.

Dan Jenkins,
sportswriter and novelist
Life Its Ownself, 1984

"You can't win, Dreamer. The owners have too much of that born-rich money behind them. They're members of the Lucky Sperm Club."

Dan Jenkins
Life Its Ownself, 1984

To quote a famous philosopher, "The exhibition season sucks." I don't even know why we play it. It's a money-making proposition for the owners, and that's it. It doesn't mean anything, and the guys know it. Everybody knows it.

Lyle Alzado,
Raiders defensive lineman
Seattle Post-Intelligencer, 1985

I've never known an owner to turn the other cheek unless he was ducking to get out of the way of a punch.

Gene Klein, former Chargers owner
First Down and a Billion, 1987

CHARLES "STORMY" BIDWELL—CARDINALS 1962–1972

Stormy decided to give his coaches psychological tests. He's the guy who needed it.

Weeb Ewbank,
former Colts and Jets coach

He would have been the greatest defensive end in the world if two ham sandwiches were painted on the helmets of all opposing quarterbacks.

> Edward Bennett Williams, Redskins
> owner, on Bidwell's weight

AL DAVIS—RAIDERS 1966–

Any society that will put [Hell's Angels leader Sonny] Barger in jail and make Al Davis a respectable millionaire at the same time is not a society to be trifled with.

> Hunter S. Thompson, writer
> *Rolling Stone,* 1974

For pure, unmitigated greed, no one on the West Coast can touch him. He's trying to move a money-making franchise out of Oakland so he can make even more money. Has the nerve to pretend it's Oakland's fault—not his. That's in very bad taste. On top of that he wants to go to L.A.—of all places. That's in even worse taste.

> Lowell Cohn, sports columnist
> *San Francisco Chronicle,* 1980

Davis is the most like James Dean of any guy I've known. Except Davis is a rebel *with* a cause.

> John Matuszak,
> Raiders defensive end
> *San Jose Mercury News,* 1981

I'd like to bury the hatchet—right between Al Davis's shoulder blades.

> Ken Stabler,
> former Raiders quarterback
> *San Jose Mercury News,* 1981

He's the kind of guy that would steal a guy's eyeballs and then tell him he looks better without them.

> Sam Rutigliano, Browns coach
> *San Francisco Chronicle,* 1981

He makes Darth Vader look like a punk.

Hunter S. Thompson, writer
Inside Sports, 1981

There are no maybes in Davis's world. No mauves, beiges, or plaids. The fact that he is partially color-blind has nothing to do with it, he insists.

Gary Smith, sportswriter
Inside Sports, 1981

Except for the Waltons and Ozzie and Harriet, every family has its crazy Uncle Harold, and among NFL owners the family embarrassment is Al Davis.

Glen Waggoner, sportswriter
Esquire, 1982

If you had a two-foot putt to close out a golf match with him, he'd be standing there jingling the change in his pocket.

Furman Bisher, sports columnist
The Sporting News, 1984

Al Davis is the kind of man who, if you spit in his face, looks up at the sky and says it must be raining.

Gene Klein, former Chargers owner
First Down and a Billion, 1987

Al usually has the look of a person who's got a problem. That's because he's usually *got* a problem.

John Madden, CBS-TV broadcaster
One Size Doesn't Fit All, 1988

LAMAR HUNT—Chiefs 1963–

One million, two million . . .

John Madden, former Raiders coach,
on Hunt learning how to count
Sports Illustrated, 1980

If he keeps going on like that, he'll be broke in 250 years.

> H. L. Hunt, oilman, on hearing his
> son Lamar was losing $1 million a
> year with the Chiefs
> *Harper's*, 1981

ROBERT IRSAY—Colts 1972–

Football's answer to George Steinbrenner.

> Robert Ward, writer
> *Gentlemen's Quarterly*, 1984

There was absolutely no way of figuring out what he was thinking about. And when Irsay finally did say something, there was no way of figuring out *why* he was thinking about it.

> Gene Klein, former Chargers owner
> *First Down and a Billion*, 1987

JOHN MECOM—Saints 1966–1985

Right now we're in year fifteen of Mecom's twenty-five-year plan.

> Buddy Diliberto,
> New Orleans sportscaster
> *Inside Sports*, 1981

He's impossible. . . . If he was getting $600 million and there was another twenty cents across the street, he'd move [the team] for it.

> A. N. Pritzker,
> Chicago hotel magnate
> *Seattle Post-Intelligencer*, 1985

JOE ROBBIE—Dolphins 1966–1990

Joe Robbie is an enigmatic man, a case study of the type of guy who would pick a fight with Bo Derek on their wedding night.

> John Underwood, sportswriter
> *Sports Illustrated*, 1981

CARROLL ROSENBLOOM—Rams 1972–1979

When he drowned in 1979, I called Ordell Braase, an old teammate, and said, "Well, the Sicilian frogmen finally got to Rosey."

> Art Donovan, former Colts defensive
> tackle on Rosenbloom's gambling
> *Fatso*, 1987

LEONARD TOSE—Eagles 1965–1985

Leonard was a very heavy gambler. Worse, he was a bad gambler. . . . Some people claimed that the real reason casinos had opened in Atlantic City was just to be close to Leonard's money.

> Gene Klein, former Chargers owner
> *First Down and a Billion*, 1987

 # PAIN AND INJURY

Hurt is in the mind. You've got to make yourself tough and you've got to play when it hurts. That's when you play best, when it hurts. If you don't want to get hurt, then don't play football. And you'd better work in the store today or else.

> Harry Lombardi, to son Vince when
> he broke his leg playing football
> as a youth

I know more about my ankles than you do.

> Joe Don Looney, Giants running
> back, refusing to let the trainer tape
> his ankles, 1964

I taped a pad to my left ankle because it hurt; I taped the other ankle as a decoy so they wouldn't know which one was injured.

> Glenn Doughty, Michigan tailback
> *Sports Illustrated*, 1969

Honey, you just can't imagine what a thrill it is to go to bed with a professional football player. Your neck's strung up and you're all tilted around, and that ice bag is sitting on your foot. I keep expecting you to hang yourself in all those contraptions.

> Bobbie Evans, to husband Norm
> Evans, offensive tackle
> *On the Line*, 1975

It didn't do any good. My neck still hurts.

> Ira Gordon, Buccaneers guard,
> after an X-ray

I can't even limp.

> Jeff Morrow, University of Minnesota
> lineman, after injuring his left ankle
> and right knee

My knees look like they lost a knife fight with a midget.

> E. J. Holub, Chiefs linebacker
> *Sports Illustrated*, 1978

You mean you walked my ass all the way out here just because you got the wind knocked out of you?

> Fred Zamberletti, Vikings trainer, to
> receiver Ahmad Rashad

Stram: Where did you get hurt?
Haynes: Right where I'm layin', Coach.

> Abner Haynes, Chiefs running back,
> to coach Hank Stram, 1981

Waking up from all of my operations.

> Tim Foley, Dolphins defensive back,
> on his most cherished memory
> *Sports Illustrated,* 1981

My kid has come to think it is natural for me to be in some kind of cast for at least six weeks of the year.

> Charlie Waters,
> former Cowboys defensive back
> *San Jose Mercury News,* 1982

My great awakening came in my second year when I got hurt and finally realized, hey, they're shooting real bullets out there.

> John Riggins, Redskins running back
> *Sport,* 1983

I got up on the rack, drained the oil, and put in some additive. That's the trouble with a make and model my age, it's hard to get parts.

> John Riggins, on his back treatment
> at age thirty-five
> *Seattle Post-Intelligencer,* 1984

There's no pain when I'm walking, but I'm not a walking back.

> Edwin Simmons, Texas tailback, on
> his knee injury
> *Sports Illustrated,* 1984

When I was a rookie, I was six-foot-three, 230 pounds. Now, I'm six-foot-two, 270. Something's very wrong.

> Bob Golic, Browns nose tackle
> *Sports Illustrated,* 1985

The next time I see a doctor, it better be for an autopsy.

> A. J. Duhe, Dolphins linebacker, after
> his fifth operation in
> eighteen months.
> *Sports Illustrated,* 1985

I don't have far to come back. I can only throw thirty or forty yards anyway. It's not like they're repairing a Porsche—more like a Volkswagen.

> Gary Danielson, Browns quarterback,
> on a shoulder injury
> *Seattle Post-Intelligencer,* 1986

The mentality of playing hurt makes you mentally tough. At least the coaches think that. I think it makes you mentally ill.

> Dexter Clinkscale,
> former Cowboys defensive back
> *The Dallas Morning News,* 1986

How am I? Fine. I lean one way and I'm five-foot-eleven. I lean the other way and I'm six feet.

> Joe Theismann, former quarterback,
> on his broken leg
> *Orlando Sentinel,* 1986

Years ago they had to do cuts on your legs. Now it's arthroscopic surgery. You see no scars on the players' knees now because they go through their rear ends.

> Bob Uecker, sportscaster
> "The Tonight Show," NBC-TV, 1986

I had a girlfriend for three years in high school, and she broke my heart. That's the only injury I've ever had.

> Kyle Rappold, Colorado nose tackle
> *San Francisco Examiner,* 1987

I never set out to hurt anybody deliberately unless it was, you know, important. Like a league game or something.

> Dick Butkus, former Bears linebacker
> *Sports Illustrated,* 1987

The greatest pain for the average professional athlete . . . is reaching for his wallet.

> Conrad Dobler, former guard
> *They Call Me Dirty,* 1988

It's amazing once you've got the ball what *fear* will make you do.

> Elroy "Crazy Legs" Hirsch,
> Rams receiver
> *Chicago Sun-Times*, 1955

The only other group I've ever dealt with who struck me as being essentially meaner than politicians are tight ends in pro football.

> Hunter S. Thompson, writer
> *Fear and Loathing on the Campaign
> Trail '72*, 1973

When it's thrown in my direction, I know it's my ball, not the man's covering me, not the ground's—but mine. I follow it into my hands with such concentration that I can see the grain. I can even see the printing. It says JSV on it—I think.

> George Sauer, Jets receiver

A guy ain't a failure until he starts blaming the weather or the quarterback or somebody else. As long as he puts the blame on hisself for those ten passes dropped, he's got a chance to drop but nine next time.

> Bum Phillips, Saints coach
> *He Ain't No Bum*, 1980

Even now, if someone spills a drink I'll catch the ice cube and tuck it away.

> Russ Francis, 49ers tight end

It was over my head. I thought, "Oh-oh. I can't go that
high." Something got me up there. It must have been God
or something.

> Dwight Clark, 49ers receiver, on
> "The Catch," which beat Dallas, 28–
> 27, in the NFC Championship Game,
> 1982

It's like running patterns in the middle of the Triborough
Bridge, trying to find a dead spot between two cars.

> Bob Trumpy, former receiver,
> on zone defenses
> *Inside Sports,* 1985

Two guys were talking about a guy who catches well in a
crowd. To me it just means he can't get open.

> James Lofton, Packers receiver
> *Sport,* 1985

CLIFF BRANCH—RAIDERS 1972–1985

His hips are so skinny his back pockets fight each other.

> John Madden, CBS-TV broadcaster
> *Hey, Wait a Minute,*
> *I Wrote a Book!,* 1984

TIM BROWN—RAIDERS 1988–

I'm not going to tell anyone he's graduated. I'll just put a
guy wearing number 81 back there to see what happens.

> Lou Holtz, Notre Dame coach
> *The Oregonian,* 1987

MEL GRAY—CARDINALS AND OKLAHOMA OUTLAWS (USFL) 1971–1984

If Mel Gray gets even with you, you're beat.

> Tom Landry, Cowboys coach,
> to his defensive backs

BOB HAYES—Cowboys and 49ers 1965–1975

I couldn't wait the extra couple of seconds with him. I couldn't look the defensive man off, because if I did he'd be out of range of my arm.

Roger Staubach,
Cowboys quarterback

The only thing in the world that could ever keep up with him was trouble. Trouble runs an 8.6 hundred.

Jim Murray, sports columnist
Los Angeles Times, 1988

TONY HILL—Cowboys 1977–1986

You ought to go to the Wizard of Oz and ask him for some courage.

Thomas "Hollywood" Henderson,
Cowboys linebacker, to Hill

ELROY "CRAZY LEGS" HIRSCH—Chicago Rockets (AAFC) and Rams 1946–1957

His crazy legs were gyrating in six different directions all at the same time.

Francis Powers, writer
Chicago Daily News, 1942

FAIR HOOKER—Browns 1969–1974

The greatest name in football.

Alex Karras, Lions defensive tackle

JOHN JEFFERSON—Chargers, Packers, and Browns 1978–1985

J.J. is the Magic Johnson of the NFL. With no J.J., the Chargers are like the Mona Lisa without a smile.

Dan Fouts, Chargers quarterback
The Sporting News, 1981

STEVE LARGENT—SEAHAWKS 1976–1989

We could triple-team him for that matter. But why embarrass three guys at once?

Darryl Rogers, Lions coach
Seattle Post-Intelligencer, 1987

PHIL McCONKEY—GIANTS AND PACKERS 1984–1988

We have a lot of fighters on this team, but we need a fight starter, and that's McConkey, five-feet-nine and fighting the other team's bench.

John Madden, broadcaster,
announcing his All-Madden Team
"Super Bowl," CBS-TV, 1986

MAX McGEE—PACKERS 1954–1967

I tried to do everything he did. It wasn't so bad on the field, but those nights killed me.

Bob Long, Packers offensive end,
1967

STANLEY MORGAN—PATRIOTS 1977–

Once Stanley catches the ball, we count to three and look for flags. If he's not already tackled, we count six.

Ron Erhardt, Patriots coach
Inside Sports, 1981

RENALDO NEHEMIAH—49ERS 1982–1984

He does not make a sound when he runs by you. It's scary.

Tom Brookshier, broadcaster
"NFL Football," CBS-TV, 1982

JERRY RICE—49ERS 1985–

If a journeyman cornerback watches Jerry Rice on film, all he can do when the lights go up is ask for help.

> Ahmad Rashad, broadcaster and
> former receiver
> *Rashad*, 1988

DEL SHOFNER—RAMS AND GIANTS 1957–1967

Del Shofner, the Giants flanker, lanky, sallow, with ulcers, . . . has been described as looking like a saxophone player after a hard one-night stand.

> George Plimpton, writer and editor
> *Paper Lion*, 1966

HENRY "GIZMO" WILLIAMS—EAGLES 1989–

I never had any confidence in him to begin with.

> Buddy Ryan, Eagles coach, when
> asked if he had lost confidence in
> Williams, 1989

KELLEN WINSLOW—CHARGERS 1979–1987

He doesn't think like a tight end. He thinks, "I'm going to catch the ball and run," while most tight ends are looking for a place to fall down.

> Pete Shaw, Giants safety
> *Sports Illustrated*, 1982

Men, we're in front, but you never know what those Cumberland players have up their sleeves. So, in the second half, go out and hit 'em clean and hit 'em hard. Don't let up.

> John W. Heisman, Georgia Tech
> coach, as his team led 126–0 at the
> half; 222–0 was the final, 1916

What is it? It is a prolate spheroid, an elongated sphere—
that is, an elongated sphere in which the outer leather cas-
ing is drawn tightly over a somewhat smaller rubber tubing.
Better to have died as a small boy than any of you to fumble
it.

John W. Heisman

Gentlemen, you are about to play football for Yale against
Harvard. Never in your lives will you do anything so important.

T. A. D. Jones, Yale coach, 1930s

Leahy: We'll start from here. I hold in my hand a football.
Now, who can tell me what this is?
Czarobski: Hey, Coach, not so fast.

Ziggy Czarobski, Notre Dame tackle,
to coach Frank Leahy, 1940s

You guys whip Notre Dame, or, so help me, I'll whip you.

Joe Schmidt, University of Pittsburgh
captain, to his players, 1952. (One
player said, "We were more scared of
Joe Schmidt than the Irish."
Pittsburgh won, 22–19.)

All those college football coaches who hold dressing room
prayers before a game should be forced to attend church
once a week.

Duffy Daugherty,
Michigan State coach, 1960s

If you think you don't hate the Rams on Thursday, let me
promise you that by Sunday you'll hate *me* so much that
you'll go out and destroy somebody.

Vince Lombardi, Packers coach

The hell with recognition through the years. Let's get the money. Let's get my car paid for.

Ray Nitschke, Packers linebacker, to
his teammates before they won a
third straight NFL title, 1967

I tell myself before a game that I'm Paul Bunyan. I wake up in the hotel room in the morning and say to myself, "Paul, we're going to have ourselves a game this afternoon. We are going to remove the stuffings from people." I can feel myself inflate.

Alex Karras, Lions defensive tackle

All I tell them about getting up for a game is that this is the only time in their lives when fifty thousand people are going to cheer them for doing something.

Joe Paterno, Penn State coach, 1968

Coach, do you want to chew us out, just for old time's sake?

Henry Jordan, Packers linebacker,
when Vince Lombardi moved up to
general manager, 1968

I give the same halftime speech over and over. It works best when my players are better than the other coach's players.

Chuck Mills, Wake Forest coach

I want my players to think as positively as the eighty-five-year-old man who married a twenty-five-year-old woman and ordered a five-bedroom house near an elementary school.

Charlie Pell, Clemson coach

All the guys kneeled down before the game to say the Lord's Prayer. When they were done everyone leaped up, put on their helmets, and charged out of the locker room screaming, "Let's kill the bastards!"

Rick Sortum, former Cardinals guard,
1970

I could make those impassioned pep talks, but I figure it's
better to keep the kids loose. I don't want to be responsible
for any suicides.

John McKay,
Southern California coach, 1974

The goal line is downfield. Run toward it, don't run toward
the sideline. You won't find anything over there but the
water bucket.

John McKay
McKay: A Coach's Story, 1975

If each of you goes out there and plays the best game you'll
ever play, if each of you plays over your head, and if each of
them plays the worst game they'll ever play, the worst game
of their lives, we still don't have a chance.

Tommy Prothro, Chargers coach,
before they lost 37–0 to the Steelers,
1975

I very rarely have ever asked a team to win a game for me,
but I'm asking you guys today because Oakland is a dirty,
cheating ball club, and I hate them.

Tommy Prothro, before losing 42–0
to the Raiders, 1976

There's not very much I can say to you. If you guys don't
play well, the Raiders are going to kick your asses.

Bud Grant, Vikings coach

Okay, men, we go to Cincinnati, we make the hit and leave
town before anyone can finger us.

Chuck Knox, Bills coach

Gentlemen, nothing funny ever happened on a football field.

Tom Landry, Cowboys coach

All they said at Albany State was "Run, run, run. Beat, beat, beat. Kill, kill, kill." When I got here, I didn't know a lot.

Mike White, Browns linebacker
San Francisco Examiner, 1980

When you get an athlete, he's got to be motivated, and he's got to be committed. It's like the kamikaze pilot who flew fifty-four missions—he was involved, but he wasn't committed.

Lou Holtz, Jets coach
"The Tonight Show," NBC-TV, 1981

The last time I [gave a fiery pre-game speech] was in high school, and the players got so stoked up they roared out of the dressing room and ran right into the basketball standard.

Bill Walsh, 49ers coach
San Jose Mercury News, 1981

I'm very familiar with hell. It's having to stand through the "Star-Spangled Banner." . . . You're bursting with adrenaline, you've just gotten a pep talk, and you have to stand there while they take nine minutes to sing a three-minute song.

Elroy "Crazy Legs" Hirsch,
former Rams receiver
San Francisco Chronicle, 1982

I told them that no matter what they did in the second half I'd still love them, and their mothers would love them—but I wasn't too sure about their girlfriends.

Sam Robertson, Southwestern
Louisiana coach, on what he told his
players at halftime as they trailed
Northeast Louisiana 26–0
The Sporting News, 1982

The first game sorta reminds me of those eighty-year-old newlyweds. We know something is gonna happen. It's just a question of when.

Bum Phillips, Saints coach,
to his players
San Francisco Examiner, 1983

You must always be prepared for today. If you lose sight of that, then you will never have a today, which was a tomorrow yesterday. What I'm saying is, you must be prepared for today, because tomorrow doesn't ever get here from yesterday, and we have to assume it will get here again tomorrow.

John Mackovic, Chiefs coach,
to his players
Sports Illustrated, 1983

Any loss is not the end of the world. If it was, you guys would have been pushing up daisies with your toes a long time ago.

Bill Snyder,
rookie Kansas State coach, 1988

Larry Roberts made one of the greatest pep talks I've ever heard. He barfed for about twenty minutes.

George Seifert, 49ers coach,
on his defensive end
San Francisco Chronicle, 1989

 **PHILOSOPHY**

Never let hope elude you. That is life's biggest fumble.

Bob Zuppke, Illinois coach

Build up your weaknesses until they become your strong points.

Knute Rockne, Notre Dame coach

The harder you work, the harder it is to surrender.

Vince Lombardi, Packers coach, 1967

Good fellows are a dime a dozen, but an aggressive leader is priceless.

Red Blaik, Army coach

We'll settle for players with three kinds of bones: a funny bone, a wishbone, and a backbone. The funny bone is to enjoy a laugh, even at one's own expense. The wishbone is to think big, set one's goals high, and to have dreams and ambitions. And the backbone—well, that's what a boy needs to get up and go to work and make all those dreams come true.

Duffy Daugherty,
Michigan State coach

Play every football game in such a way that you come off the field after a game a better player than when you went on it.

Woody Hayes, Ohio State coach

The higher you climb the flagpole, the more people see your rear end.

Don Meredith, Cowboys quarterback

Don't worry about the horse being blind, just load the wagon.

John Madden, Raiders coach, 1972

I adopted a philosophy I've never wavered from: Yesterday is a cancelled check; today is cash on the line; tomorrow is a promissory note.

Hank Stram, Chiefs coach

When you're cool the sun is always shining.

> Thomas "Hollywood" Henderson,
> Cowboys linebacker, 1975

Humility is always one play away.

> Tim Foley, Dolphins safety

Nothing happens in the game that hasn't already happened in my imagination. You have to be able to imagine yourself before you become real. Imagination is the soul of an athlete.

> Peter Gent, former Cowboys receiver
> *Texas Celebrity Turkey Trot*, 1979

The ship is sailing. It doesn't matter who you are—if you miss the boat, it goes without you.

> Jerry Burns,
> Vikings offensive coordinator

You don't know a ladder has splinters in it until you slide down it.

> Bum Phillips, Oilers coach
> *Sports Illustrated*, 1980

In society, you don't do what is just but what is possible.

> Al Davis,
> Raiders managing general partner
> *San Francisco Chronicle*, 1980

If you don't stand for something, you'll fall for anything.

> Steve Bartkowski,
> Falcons quarterback
> *Sports Illustrated*, 1981

When in doubt, sleep.

> Frank Bruno, UCLA fullback
> *Sports Illustrated*, 1981

Nothing in the world is perfect. You could get all excited about a car, but two years later there'll be a better car out.

> Herschel Walker,
> Georgia running back
> *Inside Sports*, 1981

My philosophy is: If it goes through the uprights, you're doing something right.

> Woody Woodside,
> West Virginia kicker
> *Sports Illustrated*, 1983

Enthusiasm isn't enough. The Americans had all kinds of enthusiasm at the Alamo, but the execution was awful.

> Ron Meyer, Patriots coach
> *USA Today*, 1984

An expert is an ordinary fella away from home.

> Bum Phillips, Saints coach
> *The Sporting News*, 1984

There are three types of people. . . . People who make things happen. People who watch things happen. And people who don't know what's happening.

> John Madden, CBS-TV broadcaster
> *Hey, Wait a Minute,
> I Wrote a Book!*, 1984

Just remember, happiness is having a poor memory about what happened yesterday.

> Lou Holtz, Notre Dame coach
> *Sports Illustrated*, 1985

Guys who don't wear cologne never have a sense of humor.

> John Matuszak,
> former defensive lineman
> *Cruisin' with the Tooz*, 1987

A great leader doesn't treat problems as special. He treats them as normal.

> Al Davis,
> Raiders managing general partner
> *Esquire,* 1987

A bird in the hand is always worth more than two in the bush, unless that bird craps in your hand.

> Gene Klein, former Chargers owner
> *First Down and a Billion,* 1987

The edge is a line you can live close to, but only if you know what's on the other side.

> Lawrence Taylor, Giants linebacker
> *LT: Living on the Edge,* 1987

The balls you catch, just like the ones you drop, they're only drops in a bucket, a big, big bucket.

> Ahmad Rashad, former receiver
> *Rashad,* 1988

People let you wander around in mediocrity as long as you want. But at the top of the hill, enemies await.

> Sam Wyche, Bengals coach
> *Sports Illustrated,* 1989

 **PRO LEAGUES**

CANADIAN FOOTBALL LEAGUE

I finally understood why they used twelve players up there. They keep one extra guy on the field just to pick up the fumbles.

> John David Crow,
> Cardinals running back

We had that many people selling hot dogs in the stands at Nebraska.

> Johnny Rodgers, Montreal Alouettes
> running back, on a crowd of thirteen
> thousand in the mid-1970s

NATIONAL FOOTBALL LEAGUE

I don't think I can overestimate the importance of having people continue to believe that we conduct our business with integrity, because once we have them fooled on that, we can get away with anything we want to!

> Art Modell, Browns owner, at an
> owners' meeting

Watching exhibition football is less fun than watching five hundred inexperienced kids audition for a single job in the chorus of a Broadway musical.

> Russell Baker, columnist
> *The New York Times,* 1982

NFL exhibitions, for the uninitiated, are the biggest money raisers this side of a Jerry Lewis telethon. The charity is the team ownership.

> Art Spander, sports columnist
> *The Sporting News,* 1983

If Richard Nixon had had Pete Rozelle's publicity staff, he still would be president.

> Al Davis, Raiders owner, on the NFL
> commissioner

Rozelle has an aura of power. . . . Still, I've always had a hard time trusting someone with a year-round tan who lives in New York.

> Conrad Dobler, former guard
> *They Call Me Dirty,* 1988

UNITED STATES FOOTBALL LEAGUE 1983–1985

The USFL eschewed exhibition games, undoubtedly in the belief spectators couldn't tell them from the real thing.

> Art Spander, sports columnist
> *The Sporting News*, 1983

Three years from now I believe Herschel Walker will be in a National Football League uniform. The USFL will be broke at the end of two years.

> Ray Perkins, Alabama coach
> *San Francisco Examiner*, 1983

I'd like to apologize to one person in particular, the man who won the name-the-team contest and got a lifetime pass.

> Paul Martha, Pittsburgh Maulers
> president, upon the demise of the
> team after one season
> *Sports Illustrated*, 1984

As veteran USFL watchers know, the season never heats up until the traditional Memorial Day matchups.

> Bob Costas, sportscaster
> "Major League Baseball," NBC-TV,
> 1984

I find it ironic that you put the USFL summaries on the same page as the obituaries.

> Tom Durbin, letter to the editor
> *The Sporting News*, 1985

With the Chicago Blitz, the longest lines we ever saw were of people wanting their money back. In a home game you knew you had a good hit when you could hear the echo.

> Randy Jostes, defensive tackle, 1985

Fifty-five percent of the little guys who run out on the New York streets and clean your windshield for fifty cents are USFL players.

> David Letterman
> "Late Night with David Letterman,"
> NBC-TV, 1986

There were 150 people in the courtroom—third-largest
crowd ever to see the USFL in action.

> David Letterman, on the USFL
> versus NFL antitrust trial
> "Late Night with David Letterman,"
> NBC-TV, 1986

Another day, another dollar.

> Russ Thomas, Lions general
> manager, after the USFL was
> awarded $1 in damages, 1986

WORLD FOOTBALL LEAGUE 1974–1975

I got a million-dollar offer from the World Football League.
One dollar a year for a million years.

> Steve Wright, offensive lineman

If the WFL succeeds, I'm not going after their players. I
want to sign their accountants.

> Clint Murchison, Cowboys owner,
> 1974

They're just thirty-two jerks who thought they'd be millionaires overnight. They only told us one truthful thing out of
fifty thousand lies. That was the fact we were going bank-
rupt.

> Chuck Collins,
> Detroit Wheels placekicker
> *Sports Illustrated*, 1974

You could always tell a WFL team when it gathered in a
local diner for a pre-game meal. The pep talk consisted of
three words from the team general manager: "Separate
checks, please."

> John Robertson, writer
> *McLean's*, 1975

QUARTERBACKS

Like a young god, Hercules—something like that. And the sun, the sun all around him. Remember how he waved to me? Right up from the field, with the representatives of three colleges standing by. And the buyers I brought, and the cheers when he came out—Loman, Loman, Loman! God almighty, he'll be great yet. A star like that, magnificent, can never really fade away!

Willy Loman describing his
quarterback son, Biff
Death of a Salesman by
Arthur Miller, 1949

There's a difference between a quarterback coming away from the center and saying to himself, "I hope I find my receiver," and a quarterback coming away saying, "You better stop this one, pal. I'm putting it right in his gut."

Allie Sherman, Giants coach

A quarterback hasn't arrived until he can tell the coach to go to hell.

Johnny Unitas,
former Colts quarterback

When everything else breaks down, I don't hesitate to roam out of the pocket and do the boogaloo.

Fran Tarkenton, Vikings quarterback

The quarterback dream is an American universal: Richard Nixon would give up Camp David to play quarterback for one game with the big boys.

Roger Kahn, writer
Esquire, 1971

I never made the team. . . . I was not heavy enough to play the line, not fast enough to play halfback, and not smart enough to be a quarterback.

Richard M. Nixon

Sure I think quarterbacks should be given more protection. If they want to put on a ballerina outfit and slippers. Then we won't hurt them.

Alex Karras,
former Lions defensive tackle

If you can count to eleven, you'll have no trouble playing football. Count to twenty-two and you can play quarterback.

Daryle Lamonica,
Raiders quarterback

Playing quarterback is like being in a street fight with six guys and everybody's rooting for the six.

Dan Pastorini, former quarterback

The last time I ran the ball, I got called for delay of the game.

Ken Stabler, Oilers quarterback
San Jose Mercury News, 1980

I'd like to be like them notorious quarterbacks—you know, Sonny Jurgensen or Norm Van Brocklin or Billy Kilmer— who could go out drinkin' and raisin' hell all night, then go straight to the stadium and throw about four touches. I'd like that. But me, ah'd just throw up.

Ken Stabler

How they love backup quarterbacks.

Don Meredith, former Cowboys
quarterback, on fans

The way to stay popular as a quarterback in the NFL is never to play.

> Cliff Stoudt, Steelers backup
> quarterback, 1980

Hell, a quarterback can have a few beers, and he'll get over a little headache.

> "Mean Joe" Greene, Steelers
> defensive tackle, on rule changes to
> protect quarterbacks
> *Inside Sports,* 1981

I didn't want to be a fireman or a cowboy. I stood behind the center like Unitas. I wore my facemask like Kenny Stabler. I walked hunched over like Joe Namath. I even limped like Namath. I wanted to be a quarterback.

> Joe Theismann,
> Redskins quarterback, 1983

I've known some quarterbacks who were perfectly content standing on the sideline with a telephone headset and a clipboard. Play—hell, they knew if they played, they'd blow their cover.

> John Madden, CBS-TV broadcaster
> *Hey, Wait a Minute,*
> *I Wrote a Book!,* 1984

Instead of the deep-throated *hut* I was hoping for, it came out a high-pitched *hoot,* as if someone had just squeezed my nuts.

> John Brodie, 49ers quarterback, on
> his first pro game
> *Open Field,* 1974

I should've been an all-American in bullshitting.

> Art Schlichter, Colts quarterback, on
> his gambling habit
> *Playboy,* 1984

When you're a quarterback, they love you when you're young, hate you in the middle, and love you when you're old.

> Y. A. Tittle, former quarterback
> *The Sporting News*, 1986

Scramblers are ruthless. They'd look like they were going to let you have a sack—then they'd slither away from your grasp at the moment of truth. It was like seeing your girlfriend across the bedroom in a beautiful nightgown. Then having her pass out before anything can happen.

> John Matuszak,
> former defensive lineman
> *Cruisin' with the Tooz*, 1987

My quarterback's got to be the guy who can take you in in the last two minutes, when it's getting dark and the fans are booing and the wind is blowing and there's so much ice on the ball he can't grip it.

> Charley Avedisian, high school coach

SAMMY BAUGH—REDSKINS 1937–1952

Until Sam Baugh, pro football in Texas was a one-paragraph story on the third page of the Monday sports section.

> Dan Jenkins, sportswriter
> *Sports Illustrated*, 1981

TERRY BRADSHAW—STEELERS 1970–1983

I'd always thought Terry Bradshaw the male counterpart of Ms. Anita Bryant—a rather likable and bland, harmless, intellectually vacuous Bible Belt boy who had gone to Louisiana Tech and thrown the ball well enough to make it all the way to the pros and a halftime interview.

> Frederick Exley, writer
> *Inside Sports*, 1979

Terry Bradshaw couldn't spell cat if you spotted him the "c" and the "a."

> Thomas "Hollywood" Henderson,
> Cowboys linebacker, 1979

RANDALL CUNNINGHAM—Eagles 1985–

Randall Cunningham, the elusive quarterback who often shows up where he isn't expected and rarely shows up where he is.

Ralph Wiley, sportswriter
Sports Illustrated, 1989

STEVE DeBERG—49ers, Giants, Broncos, Buccaneers, and Chiefs 1977–

He plays just well enough to get you beat.

Bill Walsh, 49ers coach

The fans booed DeBerg when he was introduced, and as it turned out, that was the high point of his night.

Douglas S. Looney, sportswriter
Sports Illustrated, 1983

JOHN ELWAY—Broncos 1983–

A Stanford coach said they had trouble finding a backup quarterback. He had to be smart enough to meet the academic qualifications of Stanford and dumb enough to play behind John Elway.

Lindsey Nelson, sportscaster
"College Football," CBS-TV, 1982

If this were England, John Elway would have been knighted by now. . . . In Moscow he'd have his own apartment. But since this is America and the NFL, the best we can offer is $1 million a year.

Paul Zimmerman, football analyst
Sports Illustrated, 1983

I didn't see the ball. I barely saw the *blur*.

Lester Hayes, Raiders cornerback, on
an Elway pass
Sports Illustrated, 1986

Got a mixing bowl haircut. Got a serious overbite—he can get the icing on the *other* side of the cake . . . he's got knock knees and a wide ass. Oh, yeah, great player. But there are just some people in this world who chemically rub you the wrong way. He does.

> Brian Bosworth, Seahawks linebacker
> *Washington*, 1988

Yeah, I guess there really *isn't* anything we can do to stop John Elway.

> Bob Golic, Browns nose guard, prior
> to losing 38–33 to Denver in the AFC
> Championship Game, 1988

JIM EVERETT—RAMS 1986–

We've been rowing across the bleepin' lake, and now we've finally gotten an outboard motor.

> John Robinson, Rams coach, upon
> drafting Everett, 1986

JOE FERGUSON—BILLS, LIONS, AND BUCCANEERS 1973–

He's been written off more times than a business lunch.

> Charlie Jones, sportscaster
> "NFL Football," CBS-TV, 1984

DOUG FLUTIE—NEW JERSEY GENERALS, BEARS, AND PATRIOTS 1985–

We put in a special formation for him—the sawed-off shotgun.

> Mike Tomczak, Bears quarterback,
> on the five-foot-nine Flutie

JOHN FOURCADE—Saints 1989–

I mean, really, to get beat by John Fourcade, who's been in every league but the Middle Eastern.

> Todd Christensen, Raiders tight end.
> (Fourcade not only played in the
> Canadian Football League and the
> United States Football League but
> also Arena Football.)
> "Sportslook," ESPN-TV, 1989

PAT HADEN—Rams 1976–1981

Pat Haden is smart enough. He didn't get that Rhodes scholarship because he ate lunch at college.

> John Madden, broadcaster
> "NFL Football," CBS-TV, 1981

BERT JONES—Colts and Rams 1973–1983

I love Bert Jones as much as my wife. . . . Would I trade my wife?

> Robert Irsay, Colts owner, 1981

I'm gonna run his ass out of town.

> Robert Irsay, 1982

SONNY JURGENSEN—Eagles and Redskins 1957–1974

If you took a survey of most quarterbacks, you'd find that they go to the Presbyterian Church and the cafeteria afterward. . . . They're all milk drinkers, and they're all alike . . . pretty boys, all in the same image. The only one I know who isn't is Sonny Jurgensen.

> Alex Karras, Lions defensive tackle

BERNIE KOSAR—Browns 1985–

He scrambles with the grace and speed of a giraffe on Quaaludes.

Jenny Kellner, sportswriter
Miami News, 1985

Gary Danielson believes Bernie Kosar is the Browns quarterback of the future. He just doesn't believe the future is now.

Jean Fugett, broadcaster
"NFL Football," CBS-TV, 1985

TOMMY KRAMER—Vikings 1977–

Kramer? He just bops along. He's not a contemplator of the world. It's hard for me to imagine how anyone can glide through life like that.

Dennis Swilley, Vikings center
Inside Sports, 1981

DAVE KRIEG—Seahawks 1980–

What is it about this guy that keeps fans from worshiping him? Probably the same thing that led his teammates to nickname him "Mudbone."

Fred Moody, sportswriter
Fighting Chance, 1989

BOBBY LAYNE—Bears, New York Browns, Lions, and Steelers 1948–1962

He never lost a game in his life. Once in a while time ran out on him.

Doak Walker, former Lions teammate

When he got on the field, it was *his* field. He owned it.

Alex Karras,
former Lions defensive tackle
Even Big Guys Cry, 1977

In my next life I'd like to come back as Bobby Layne's chauffeur because he stays out late, visits interesting places, and tips great.

> Don Meredith,
> former Cowboys quarterback

He went grocery shopping and he thought he was the best shopper in the store.

> William Andrews, former Texas
> roommate, 1986

He called one Tuesday night to have a drink and we didn't get home until Saturday.

> Frank Gifford,
> former Giants running back

Bobby didn't miss much in life. Wherever there was a drink to be drunk, a dance to be hoofed, a song to be sung, a crap shoot to fade, a horse to be bet, a card to be dealt, Bobby sat in. . . . For Bobby, life was all fast Layne.

> Jim Murray, sports columnist
> *Los Angeles Times*, 1986

NEIL LOMAX—CARDINALS 1981–1989

Neil Lomax soon will be entering his seventeenth year as quarterback of the future.

> Mike Downey, sports columnist
> *The Sporting News*, 1986

ARCHIE MANNING—SAINTS, OILERS, AND VIKINGS 1971–1984

He was a franchise player without a franchise.

> Hank Stram, sportscaster, on
> Manning's lousy teams
> *The Sporting News*, 1985

JIM McMAHON—BEARS AND CHARGERS 1982–

The day he stepped out of that limo with the beer can, I said to myself, "Well, he's sure not out to impress *me*."

Mike Ditka, Bears coach
Newsweek, 1985

He's playing with a full deck, but he's got both jokers in there.

Brian Bosworth, Oklahoma linebacker
San Francisco Examiner, 1986

It's questionable whether the brash, cocky, outspoken Mc-Mahon could have played quarterback for George Halas. He looks very much like a young man whose car hood never cools off.

John Owen, sports columnist
Seattle Post-Intelligencer, 1986

If it weren't for football, he'd be some yo-yo out here drinking beer.

Joe Theismann, former quarterback,
1986 (McMahon replied to
Theismann's comment, "Who is he to
talk? He left his wife and kids.")

If you can't figure him out, don't ask me. He has been a mystery since Day One.

Roberta McMahon, Jim's mother
The Sporting News, 1986

He celebrates a touchdown by head-butting his teammates. Jim McMahon supplies what I call "good goofy," a spirit that every team needs.

John Madden, CBS-TV broadcaster
One Size Doesn't Fit All, 1988

DON MEREDITH—Cowboys 1960–1968

Meredith: What do you think Tom Landry *really* thinks of me?

Perkins: I think Landry wishes you had never been born.

> Don Meredith and Dallas sportswriter
> Steve Perkins, on the Cowboys coach,
> 1968

JOE MONTANA—49ers 1979–

Who is this, the *punter?*

> Dwight Clark, 49ers receiver, upon
> first meeting Montana, 1979

Small children fight for his autograph and grown women swoon over his blond good looks, the alpine blue of his eyes, the shy grin that makes you look to see if he's modestly scuffing a toe in the dust.

> Jerry Carroll, staff writer
> *San Francisco Chronicle,* 1984

His record in big games is better than John Wayne's in movie shootouts.

> Allen Barra, sportswriter
> *Inside Sports,* 1985

Joe Montana is as cool as the other side of the pillow.

> Wayne Walker, 49ers broadcaster
> KGO-Radio, San Francisco, 1989

JOE NAMATH—Jets and Rams 1965–1977

I knew I was on to something special the first time I visited him in Beaver Falls. When I took him out to dinner, while he was still in high school, he ordered bourbon and water.

> Tom Nugent, Maryland coach, 1962

If Mark Twain had lived in Beaver Falls and had known Joe Namath, nobody would have heard of Tom Sawyer.

> Beano Cook, football analyst, 1969

You won't find long hair or sideburns à la Joe Namath here.
There are no hippies in the FBI.

J. Edgar Hoover, FBI director, 1970

The idea of little boys and girls hero-worshiping Joe Namath
was enough to make William Buckley's eyebrows quiver
with fear for the decline of Western civilization.

Larry Merchant, sportswriter
*And Every Day You Take Another
Bite,* 1971

Why did Joe Namath become such a national hero? Because
deep down in our hearts *we* wanted all those broads.

Maury Allen, sportswriter
The New Yorker, 1979

GIFFORD NIELSEN—Oilers 1978–1983

In the huddle I can't get used to the smell of milkshakes on
Gifford's breath.

Carl Mauck, Oilers center, when
Nielsen replaced Ken Stabler
San Francisco Chronicle, 1981

DAN PASTORINI—Oilers, Raiders, Rams, and Eagles 1971–1983

He's just six-foot-three and he's strong; he's perfectly condi-
tioned and has a good tan and he has long hair, and he's
pretty the way a quarterback's supposed to be. Alex Karras
would hate him.

Bill Curry, Packers center

MILT PLUM—Browns, Lions, Rams, and Giants 1957–1969

Plum was never a great quarterback with the Lions, however gifted. . . . He was destroyed by his name. His parents
probably wanted him to play the cello.

Alex Karras, Lions defensive tackle

BOBBY SCOTT—Saints and Arizona Wranglers (USFL)

He wanted nothing to do with the starting job, wanted nothing to do with all of the pressures and demands that came with it. He was afraid they might interfere with his beer drinking.

Conrad Dobler, former guard
They Call Me Dirty, 1988

BRIAN SIPE—Browns and New Jersey Generals (USFL) 1974–1985

Sipe has won more games with people booing him than any quarterback in the NFL.

Sam Rutigliano, Browns coach
The Sporting News, 1983

STEVE SPURRIER—49ers and Buccaneers 1967–1976

Spurrier back to pass. It's deflected. But then again, maybe it wasn't.

Lon Simmons, 49ers broadcaster

KEN STABLER—Raiders, Oilers, and Saints 1970–1984

Stabler frequently left his game in some parked car the night before.

Bear Bryant, Alabama coach

His motto is that of a man whose main worry in life is that he might miss something while driving between saloons.

Pete Axthelm, sportswriter
Inside Sports, 1980

I'd like to be like the Snake. . . . All that gray hair, throwing sidearm until they kick me out of the league.

Joe Montana, 49ers quarterback
San Francisco Examiner, 1987

He's the only guy I knew who, on Game Day, looked worse in person than he did in the photograph on his driver's license.

> Conrad Dobler, former guard, on
> Stabler's many hits
> *They Call Me Dirty*, 1988

ROGER STAUBACH—Cowboys 1969–1979

Roger Staubach, commenting on CBS-TV on the Pittsburgh rush: "They're coming heck-bent for leather." Now, *that's* really straight arrow.

> Glenn Dickey, sports columnist
> *San Francisco Chronicle*, 1980

FRAN TARKENTON—Vikings and Giants 1961–1978

I've never caught him yet.

> "Mean Joe" Greene,
> Steelers defensive tackle, 1974

Y. A. TITTLE—Colts, 49ers, and Giants 1948–1964

"Without Tittle," said my neighbor in the stands, "the Giants couldn't go from Grand Central to Times Square on the subway."

> Irwin Shaw, writer
> *Esquire*, 1965

JOHNNY UNITAS—Colts and Chargers 1956–1974

I swear that when he sees you coming out of the corner of his eye, he holds that ball a split second longer than he really needs to—just to let you know he isn't afraid of any man.

> Merlin Olsen, Rams defensive tackle

We should've won, but Unitas is a guy who knows what it was to eat potato soup seven days a week as a kid. That's what beat us.

> Norm Van Brocklin, Rams coach,
> losing to the Colts
> in the final minutes

Unitas led his team down the field three times, like a man walking his dog.

> Jim Marshall, Vikings defensive end,
> when Unitas rallied the Colts from
> twenty points down to win

You could be yelling at him, and he never even looked at you. He had no reaction at all. At least not until he completed the pass. Then he gave you that smile. That damn smile.

> Dick Butkus, former Bears linebacker
> *The New York Times,* 1979

NORM VAN BROCKLIN—RAMS AND EAGLES 1949–1960

When he tried to run, it was just like a man running in place. His legs moved, but he never went anywhere.

> John McKay,
> Southern California coach
> *McKay: A Coach's Story,* 1975

His running style once was characterized as "like a woman trying to get out of her girdle."

> Furman Bisher, sports columnist
> *The Sporting News,* 1983

BOB WATERFIELD—BROWNS AND RAMS 1945–1952

I think Waterfield could have played another five years, but he finally got tired of the booing.

> Don Klosterman, former Rams
> general manager
> *Sports Illustrated,* 1981

DANNY WHITE—COWBOYS 1976–1988

The guy's got a year's supply of dried food in his basement.
He's got phone numbers to call when Armageddon arrives.
That's the kind of guy you want quarterbacking your team,
down seventeen points with the time running down?

> Peter Gent, former Cowboys receiver,
> 1983

His numbers are slightly higher than Staubach's. But I can
close my eyes and see Staubach putting the ball on the
money twenty yards downfield, and when I think of White I
see an eight-yard completion on third-and-ten.

> Paul Zimmerman, football analyst
> *The New Thinking Man's Guide to
> Pro Football*, 1984

DOUG WILLIAMS—BUCCANEERS, OKLAHOMA OUTLAWS (USFL), AND REDSKINS 1978–

Doug Williams needs one more season of target practice—
the joke last year was that he was the one man who could
overthrow the Ayatollah.

> Gary Smith, sportswriter
> *Inside Sports*, 1980

He never throws a change-up. Every pitch is a fastball.

> John Madden, broadcaster
> "NFL Football," CBS-TV, 1988

MARC WILSON—RAIDERS AND PATRIOTS 1980–

He's not a bad player. He just doesn't belong with the Raiders. He belongs with Dallas, where everybody's Goody Two-
Shoes.

> Jim McMahon, Bears quarterback
> *Time*, 1986

No one adds more suspense to a game than Wilson. He is one of the great mountains of indecision in the world of sport today. You watch Marc Wilson play football, and you wonder how he gets himself dressed in the morning. You'd think if you handed him a menu, he'd starve to death.

> Jim Murray, sports columnist
> *Los Angeles Times,* 1986

 RECRUITING AND DRAFTING

When I'm traveling I ask farm boys how to get to a certain place. If they point with their finger, I move on. If they pick up the plow and point with it, I stop and sell them on the University of Minnesota.

> Gil Dobie, University of Minnesota
> alumnus and recruiter, 1920

They tell me I should go around kissing babies and talking to mothers of poor boys to persuade them to send their sons to Illinois. . . . I told them that if that was the duty of a modern coach, then I wasn't capable of being a modern coach.

> Bob Zuppke, Illinois coach, 1929

Recruiting is like wining and dining the girl you're gonna marry.

> Pepper Rodgers, Georgia coach

Any kid who would leave that wonderful weather is too dumb to play for us.

> Alex Agase, Purdue coach, on why he
> does not recruit in California

I don't acknowledge smog. It hurts recruiting.

Terry Donahue, UCLA coach
The Sporting News, 1983

Our grants-in-aid are based on academic achievement and need. By academic achievement we mean can the boy read and write. By need—well, we don't take a boy unless we need him.

Duffy Daugherty,
Michigan State coach

It's like a beauty contest. It's easy to pick out the top one, two, or three girls. But then the rest of them look the same.

Gil Brandt,
Cowboys head of personnel

I'll say one thing for them—computers never try to sell you their brother-in-law as a prospect.

Gil Brandt

Never praise a draft choice too much until he's signed.

Al Davis,
Raiders managing general partner

I know how you recruit—with $100 bills. If they'd make me a coach in college, we'd win, then we'd be on probation, then we'd win again, then we'd be on probation again, then we'd win again, then we'd be on probation again.

Bobby Layne,
former Lions quarterback
Playboy, 1982

He was one of them twenty-footers. All you had to see was twenty feet of film and you wanted him.

Fred Akers, Texas coach, on running
back Gerald Sims
Sports Illustrated, 1982

I actually took a cut in pay when I went from the University of Washington to the San Francisco 49ers as a rookie—and that's the truth.

> Hugh McElhenny,
> former running back, 1982

If a stranger shows up in this town (Philadelphia, Mississippi), they ain't lookin' for nobody but Marcus.

> Cella Dupree Connors, running back
> Marcus Dupree's mother,
> on recruiters
> *Sports Illustrated*, 1983

Recruiting is the key. Shoot, Barnum & Bailey wouldn't have a circus without the lions, tigers, elephants, and giraffes.

> Ray Alborn, Rice coach
> *Inside Sports*, 1983

I think they drafted in alphabetical order.

> Brent Ziegler, Syracuse fullback
> picked 265th in the NFL draft
> *Sports Illustrated*, 1984

When I bring in a player, I take him out for a big sparerib dinner, show him Memphis, and take him to my big ol' house overlooking the beautiful Mississippi. Then I ask him, "Boy, do you *really* want to play in *Buffalo?*"

> Pepper Rodgers,
> Memphis Showboats coach
> *Sport*, 1985

Sleepers don't often wake up.

> Don James,
> University of Washington coach
> *Seattle Post-Intelligencer*, 1985

Recruiting . . . makes me feel like a pimp. You would be appalled at the things I have to do to recruit. A man my age.

> Bo Schembechler, Michigan coach
> *Bo,* 1989

 **RETIREMENT**

When a guy who couldn't run one hundred yards in twenty seconds caught me from behind, I walked off the field and quit the next day.

> Red Grange,
> former Bears running back

The older you get, the faster you ran when you were a kid.

> Steve Owen, Giants coach

Damn it, I'm not getting mellow. . . . The minute I think I'm getting mellow, then I'm retiring. Who ever heard of a mellow winner?

> Woody Hayes, Ohio State coach, after
> a losing season, 1966

I knew it was time to quit when I was chewing out an official and he walked off the penalty faster than I could keep up with him.

> George Halas, former Bears coach

Then one year he jumps on your back. Sometimes you can brush him off, but every year he gets heavier and grips harder. I've seen him riding the backs of others. He's right around here somewhere. Look yonder—he might be beyond the door. Maybe he's behind that curtain over there.

> Bubba Smith, defensive lineman, on
> getting older and facing "The Monkey"

I've got one advantage: When you're as slow as I am, you don't lose any steps as you grow older.

> Howard Twilley, Dolphins receiver

Spending time with your family is overrated. You go to spend time with your family, and they really don't have time to spend with you. . . . I wound up sitting around the house by myself.

> John Madden, former Raiders coach
> *Inside Sports,* 1980

Not me. I haven't been gone long enough to forget what the pain feels like.

> Willie Alexander, former Oilers
> defensive back, when asked if he
> would consider a comeback
> *Sports Illustrated,* 1983

Ninety-five percent of me is very sad. But my knees—the other five percent—are very, very happy.

> Dan Dierdorf, Cardinals offensive
> lineman, announcing his retirement,
> *The Sporting News,* 1983

It's strange to be unemployed, but at least I can't blame it on the Japanese.

> Doug Plank, former Bears safety
> *The Sporting News,* 1983

My big fear is where am I going to find a job with a six-month vacation.

> John Riggins, Redskins running back
> *Sport,* 1983

Phillips: Ken Stabler is like Earl Campbell. He may not be in a class by himself, but it doesn't take long to call the roll.
Reporter: That's an old quote.
Phillips: That's an old quarterback.

> Bum Phillips, Oilers coach
> *USA Today,* 1983

No wonder Ken Stabler retired. In the picture that went with the story, Stabler looked like Howard Hughes—just before Hughes died.

> Glenn Dickey, sports columnist
> *San Francisco Chronicle*, 1984

After twelve years the old butterflies came back. Well, I guess at my age you call them moths.

> Franco Harris, Seahawks running
> back, age thirty-four
> *Seattle Post-Intelligencer*, 1984

You're always building something, and the time goes by on you, Hoss. The thing you think about is that one day you might wake up and realize that the whole time you were building something, that was the time you had it all.

> Terry Bradshaw, Steelers quarterback
> *Esquire*, 1984

I'm going to tuck a football under my arm and head south of the border. When I get far enough south for someone to ask, "What's that thing you're carrying?" that's where I'm going to retire.

> Ed Doherty, Arizona coach

I really just have to see a picture of the Chicago Bears once a week, and I don't miss anything.

> Archie Manning,
> former quarterback
> *The Sporting News*, 1985

I'm walking around with this huge body and don't know what to do with it.

> Tom Condon, 280-pound guard
> released by the Chiefs
> *USA Today*, 1985

I don't know if they're my memories or remains, but I wouldn't trade any of this for a fresh-stocked whorehouse in Texas.

> Ken Stabler, former quarterback,
> surveying his trophies and
> mementos, 1985

After eighteen years in the trenches, it's just time to get out of football. I need to get into something serious, another career. Maybe pro wrestling.

> Jeff Van Note, Falcons center, 1986

Probably the Beatles' white album.

> Steve Largent, Seahawks receiver,
> when asked what record he would
> treasure most, 1987

The real difficulty with retirement is that you never know when you're finished.

> Gene Klein, former Chargers owner
> *First Down and a Billion,* 1987

RUNNING BACKS

There is still no thrill comparable to the one furnished by a fast, shifty, elusive runner who tucks that wind-jammed pig rind under his arm and swivel-hips his way through a broken field to climax his effort by crossing the goal line standing up.

> Paul Gallico, sportswriter

The qualifications for a lineman are to be big and dumb. To be a back you only have to be dumb.

> Knute Rockne, Notre Dame coach

Doc was raised to be a football hero. At four he was hit by a truck, but the broken leg didn't slow him down, and the truck never ran again.

> John T. Brady,
> on Army's Doc Blanchard
> *The Heisman: A Symbol of*
> *Excellence,* 1984

If you're good enough, you're big enough.

> Woody Hayes, Ohio State coach,
> upon meeting 175-pound Howard
> "Hopalong" Cassady, 1952

When you get through a hole, don't run out there like a mule in the twenty-acre pasture. Look for *friends*.

> Jack Curtice, Stanford coach, on
> using blockers

Forrest Evashevski always told you the first thing that he was the blocking back in the Michigan backfield who'd made Tom Harmon great. That always goes in the first or second minute of conversation, whether he was talking to a thirteen-year-old kid or a grandmother in her nineties.

> Alex Karras, Lions defensive tackle

Nothing, not a tank, not a wall, not a dozen men can stop you from getting across that goal line. If I ever see one of my backs get stopped a yard from the goal line, I'll come off that bench and kick him right in the ass.

> Vince Lombardi, Packers coach, 1967

Anyone can run where the holes are. A good football player makes his own holes.

> Joe Don Looney, former running
> back
> *Sports Illustrated,* 1970

I wasn't much good. When I went into the line on a fake, I would holler, "I don't have it!"

> Bob Newhart, comedian, on his high
> school career

If you were a kid who loved to have people chase you,
you've got the beginnings of a running back.

> Larry Csonka, Dolphins running
> back, 1969

I'm cool on the outside, but inside it's like a thousand little
kids jumping up and down on Christmas morning.

> Chuck Foreman, Vikings running
> back, on scoring a touchdown

I would like the body of Jim Brown, the moves of Gale Sayers, the strength of Earl Campbell, and the acceleration of
O. J. Simpson. Just once I would like to run and feel the
wind in my hair.

> Rocky Bleier, Steelers running back
> *San Francisco Chronicle*, 1979

It's the most lonely feeling in the world breaking into day-
light and knowing you still have eighty yards to go.

> Kenny King, Raiders running back,
> on an eighty-nine-yard touchdown
> run
> *The New York Times*, 1980

The breakaway backs *never* block after the first year. They
let you know they're there for other things.

> Bill Walsh, 49ers coach
> *San Francisco Chronicle*, 1981

The hole is never where it's supposed to be.

> Franco Harris, Steelers running back
> *Sports Illustrated*, 1982

There are three types of runners. Runners like Gary Anderson, they run between trees. Runners like Jessie Clark, they
run over the trees. The type we have, they run into the
trees.

> Lou Holtz, Arkansas coach
> *San Francisco Examiner*, 1983

Trying to compare running backs is like trying to draw the wind.

> Walter Payton, Bears running back
> *USA Today,* 1984

If you have the football and eleven guys are after you, if you're smart, you'll run. It was no big deal.

> Red Grange, former running back
> *Sports Illustrated,* 1985

The way I figure it, if some guy's bigger than me, then he's not as fast, and if he's as fast—then I guess it's about time for me to get out of the league.

> Lionel James, Chargers running back
> *Sports Illustrated,* 1985

MARCUS ALLEN—RAIDERS 1982–

I throw a block and feel a brush of air go by me. It's Marcus.

> Kenny King, Raiders fullback
> *San Francisco Chronicle,* 1983

Marcus does for football what Dolly Parton does for a sweater. He makes you sit up and take notice.

> Charlie Jones, broadcaster
> "NFL Football," NBC-TV, 1984

ROCKY BLEIER—STEELERS 1968–1980

Rocky gained 1,036 yards in 1976 without ever making a cut.

> Ray Mansfield, Steelers center

JIM BROWN—BROWNS 1956–1965

Jim Brown, in one ninety-yard run yesterday, taught George Preston Marshall the wisdom of being color-blind.

> Shirley Povich, sportswriter, on the
> Redskins owner
> *The Washington Post*

LEON BURNS—Chargers and Cardinals 1971–1972

Leon Burns came out of prison. . . . He used to wear a Superman T-shirt under his uniform. After watching him play, I assumed he had gone to jail for false advertising.

> Gene Klein, former Chargers owner
> *First Down and a Billion*, 1987

EARL CAMPBELL—Oilers and Saints 1978–1985

When you tackle him, it sure reduces your IQ.

> Pete Wysocki, Redskins linebacker
> *San Francisco Chronicle*, 1979

Maybe what I'll do is have them jump offside every play. That way, they only get five yards at a time, and Earl's averaging 5.7 yards a carry.

> Bum Phillips, Saints coach, when
> Campbell was with Houston
> *San Francisco Examiner*, 1981

I remember calling Earl one time and saying, "Why don't you let one man tackle you sometime?"

> Tony Dorsett, Cowboys running back
> *Sports Illustrated*, 1986

LARRY CSONKA—Dolphins, Memphis Southmen (WFL), and Giants 1968–1979

When he goes on safari, the lions roll up their windows.

> Monte Clark, Lions coach
> *Sports Illustrated*, 1979

I was trying to tackle Larry Csonka around the ankles, but he was carrying so many of our men, I was afraid I'd hit a teammate.

> Doug Plank, Bears safety
> *San Francisco Examiner*, 1979

SAM "THE BAM" CUNNINGHAM—PATRIOTS 1973–1981

I made him a blocker for three years. He's the best runner I ever ruined.

> John McKay, Southern California
> coach, after Cunningham scored four
> touchdowns in the Rose Bowl, 1973

ERIC DICKERSON—RAMS AND COLTS 1983–

If he gets two strides on you, the next guy in motion is the scoreboard operator.

> F. A. Dry, Texas Christian coach

Dickerson's sense of commitment is like a parking meter. It's fine as long as you feed it money every twelve minutes.

> Tony Kornheiser, sportswriter, on
> Dickerson's contract renegotiations
> *The Washington Post,* 1987

The defender is moving with the play when . . . uh-oh—he realizes that he's lost the angle on Eric. Checkmate.

> Ahmad Rashad,
> former Vikings receiver
> *Rashad,* 1988

TONY DORSETT—COWBOYS AND BRONCOS 1977–1989

T. D. is quicker than a hiccup and tougher than week-old bread.

> Harry Jones, University of Pittsburgh
> backfield coach, 1976

Tony made life awfully easy for me. I just handed off to him and watched the game.

> Danny White, Cowboys quarterback
> *Chicago Sun-Times,* 1981

HOWIE FERGUSON—Packers and Los Angeles Chargers 1953–1960

Ferguson was very much like Packers fullback Jimmy Taylor, except that he didn't have Taylor's ability.

Sid Gillman, Chargers coach

MIKE GARRETT—Chiefs and Chargers 1966–1973

He eats more dirt than a gopher. His throat has the fingerprints of every linebacker in the league on it.

Jim Murray, sports columnist
Los Angeles Times, 1965

WALT GARRISON—Cowboys 1966–1974

If you needed four yards, you could give the ball to Walt and he'd get you four yards. If you needed twenty yards, you could give the ball to Walt and he'd get you four yards.

Don Meredith,
former Cowboys quarterback
Seattle Post-Intelligencer, 1985

FRANK GIFFORD—Giants 1952–1964

For his whole life, whenever Gifford has walked into a room, he has been the coolest guy in the room. Most of us don't know what that's like.

Bob Greene, journalist
Esquire, 1983

Yesterday he had on a pair of Levi's and a T-shirt with "Mama" written on it. I had on a five-hundred-dollar suit. I looked like Emmett Kelly, and he looked like a guy in a tuxedo.

Alex Karras, Gifford's former
broadcasting partner
Esquire, 1983

FRANCO HARRIS—Steelers and Seahawks 1972– 1984

He faked me out so bad one time I got a fifteen-yard penalty for grabbing my own facemask.

> D. D. Lewis, Dallas linebacker
> *The New York Times,* 1979

PAUL HORNUNG—Packers 1957–1966

You know what made him great inside the five-yard line like no other player? *He loved the glory.* . . . He loved the glory like no other player I've ever coached.

> Vince Lombardi, Packers coach, 1969

EARNEST JACKSON—Chargers, Eagles, and Steelers 1983–1988

Get him out of here. Trade him for a six-pack. It doesn't have to be cold.

> Buddy Ryan, Eagles coach, at
> practice before Jackson was cut, 1986

PETE JOHNSON—Bengals, Chargers, and Dolphins 1977–1984

Pete Johnson . . . is not really a football player but a garbage truck in pads.

> Lowell Cohn, sports columnist
> *San Francisco Chronicle,* 1982

JOE DON LOONEY—Colts, Lions, Redskins, and Saints 1964–1969

Joe Don Looney: Never was a man more aptly named.

> George Sauer, former Jets receiver

TOM MATTE—Colts 1961–1972

He wasn't supposed to be fast enough, but he never realized that.

> Bill Curry, former center

HUGH McELHENNY—49ERS, VIKINGS, GIANTS, AND LIONS 1952–1964

People used to argue about his touchdown runs the way two guys on a beach argue about girls. The last one to pass by is always the prettiest.

> Mickey Herskowitz, sportswriter
> *The Golden Age of Pro Football,* 1974

TERRY METCALF—CARDINALS, TORONTO ARGONAUTS (CFL), AND REDSKINS 1973–1981

Other guys would go crying to the official. Metcalf would take care of you personally.

> Thomas "Hollywood" Henderson,
> former linebacker
> *Out of Control,* 1987

JOE MORRIS—GIANTS 1982–

A flashbulb has about as much chance of catching him as a linebacker.

> Mark Whicker, sportswriter, 1986

MARION MOTLEY—BROWNS AND STEELERS 1946–1955

You rush quarterback Otto Graham and put on a move and beat your man, and there's Motley waiting for you. Next play, you beat your man with a different move, and there's Motley waiting again. Pretty soon you say, "The hell with it. I'd rather stay on the line and battle the first guy."

> Gail Bruce, defensive lineman

CHUCK MUNCIE—SAINTS AND CHARGERS 1976–1984

He went to five grandmothers' funerals.

> Bum Phillips, Saints coach, on
> Muncie's excuses
> *San Francisco Chronicle,* 1984

I usually sat . . . next to running back Chuck Muncie. After all, somebody had to wake him up when the films came on.

Conrad Dobler, former Saints
teammate
They Call Me Dirty, 1988

BRONKO NAGURSKI—Bears 1930–1937, 1943

He was the only man I ever saw who ran his own interference.

Steve Owen, former Giants coach

I stared at him, bug-eyed. Hell, I knew more about him than *he* did.

Alex Karras, Lions defensive tackle,
on meeting his childhood hero

DARRIN NELSON—Vikings 1982–1988

The first time I saw Darrin Nelson run, I realized this was the kind of player who causes some coaches to keep their jobs—and some to lose theirs.

Paul Wiggin, former Stanford coach
San Francisco Chronicle, 1980

WALTER PAYTON—Bears 1975–1987

When Walter went down the assembly line, everything was chrome-plated.

Clyde Emrich, Bears strength coach
USA Today, 1984

Walter Payton runs like a Tasmanian Devil. He growls.

John Robinson, Rams coach
Sport, 1986

JOHN RIGGINS—Jets and Redskins 1971–1985

He signed the contract sitting at the desk in my office. He had that Mohawk haircut, and he was stripped to the waist and wearing leather pants and a derby hat with a feather in it. It must have been what the sale of Manhattan Island looked like.

> Weeb Ewbank, former Jets coach
> *Sports Illustrated*, 1983

BARRY SANDERS—LIONS 1989–

He can fly through a keyhole.

> Barry Switzer, Oklahoma coach
> *Los Angeles Times*, 1988

GALE SAYERS—BEARS 1965–1971

It looks like he's not running fast, but nobody is gaining on him.

> Bill Curry, Packers center

O. J. SIMPSON—BILLS AND 49ERS 1969–1979

They say his nickname is Orange Juice. But the O.J. ought to stand for Oh, Jesus, as in "Oh, Jesus, there he goes again."

> Roger Valdiserri, Notre Dame head of
> publicity, 1967

It's like watching a drunk run through traffic on a freeway. You don't have to know the game to appreciate O.J.'s act—it's a spectacle, a thing to see.

> Hunter S. Thompson, writer
> *Scanlan's Monthly*, 1970

I was tempted more than once to sign autographs: "John McKay, friend of O. J. Simpson."

> John McKay,
> Southern California coach
> *McKay: A Coach's Story*, 1975

O.J. never really did belong in Buffalo. He was a Maserati in a snowplow town.

Gary Smith, sportswriter
Inside Sports, 1981

JIM THORPE—GIANTS 1929

It was as if a locomotive had hit me and been followed by a ten-ton truck rambling over the remains.

Knute Rockne, Notre Dame coach,
trying to tackle Thorpe

WENDELL TYLER—RAMS AND 49ERS 1977–1986

What I remember most about Wendell is he always played us with a little grin on his face as he ran by.

Bill Walsh, 49ers coach
Sport, 1983

HERSCHEL WALKER—NEW JERSEY GENERALS (USFL), COWBOYS, AND VIKINGS 1983–

I saw him running, got in front of him, and waited for him to make a move, left or right. Instead, he ran over me.

Billy Bates, Tennessee safety, 1980

We didn't coach him, we just aimed him.

Gary Phillips,
Walker's Georgia high school coach
The Sporting News, 1982

We'll toss him the ball and point him north.

Chuck Fairbanks,
New Jersey Generals coach
USA Today, 1983

 SPECIAL TEAMS

I swung my leg mightily—took out a big divot—and kicked a low line drive that hit Bulldog Turner right in the hind end. And up in the broadcast booth I understand Jack Brickhouse hollered, "Watch it now—the Bears got a trick play."

> George "Moose" Connors, when as rookie in 1948 Bears coach George Halas asked him to try a field goal

I can't stand those little jerks. They come in singing their little song, "I am go-eng to keek a touchdown; I am go-eng to keek a touchdown."

> Alex Karras, Lions defensive tackle, on foreign-born kickers

Lord, don't ever phone me the day after a game. I'll either be still getting drunk or lookin' for bail. When you're on a suicide team like I am, you don't wait till next week to start living.

> Mike Battle, Jets kick returner

I tell him, "Learn me the rules, learn me the English language, but don't learn me how to kick."

> Toni Fritsch, Cowboys placekicker, to coach Tom Landry, 1971

McDonough: Gene Upshaw wants to receive. What are you going to do?
Jones: I am going to whip his ass all over the field.

> Deacon Jones, Chargers defensive end, to official John McDonough at the coin toss, 1973

I'm not a football player. I'm a punter.

> Dave Jennings, Giants punter, 1979

Everyone has some fear. A man who has no fear belongs in a mental institution. Or on special teams.

Walt Michaels, Jets coach
Sports Illustrated, 1979

It's like embalming. Nobody likes to, but someone has to.

Ted Watts, Raiders kick returner
San Francisco Examiner, 1981

Returning punts is not a job I can get excited about. Most of the things that can happen to you are negative. One, you can fumble. Two, you can get slammed down in your tracks. Three, you can come up fast on a punt and run into your own man. Four, you can be second-guessed for not signaling for a fair catch. And five, you can get a concussion. You risk all this for maybe eight yards.

Roland Hooks, Bills running back
TV Guide, 1982

We need to start teaching geography a few years earlier.

Al Antak, Camas (Washington) High
School coach, when his punt returner
ran fifty-four yards the wrong way for
a safety
Sports Illustrated, 1983

Your teammates are the blood and sweat; you're the tears.

Eddie Murray, Lions placekicker
Pro Football Weekly, 1984

That's the way my whole career's been: a foot-and-a-half right.

Gary Danielson, Lions quarterback
and placekick holder
Sports Illustrated, 1984

My parents sent me to Harvard to become a specialist. I don't think they were thinking of this.

Pat McInally, Bengals punter, 1984

An NFL game today is like a golf tournament in which you play your way up to the green and find a guy from Brazil standing there to do the putting for you.

Norm Pollom, Bills scout
Sports Illustrated, 1985

People don't think of me as Rich Karlis, the guy who kicks 80 percent. They think of me as the guy who always hits uprights.

Rich Karlis, Denver placekicker
Seattle Post-Intelligencer, 1985

My helmet was too tight and it was squeezing my brain. I couldn't think.

Raphael Septien, Dallas placekicker,
on why he missed a field goal, 1985

No wonder. You placed the ball upside down.

Raphael Septien, missing another
field goal, to holder Danny White,
1985

Lots of guys can kick in their underwear in practice.

John Madden, CBS-TV broadcaster
One Knee Equals Two Feet, 1986

Going to a professional football game expecting to see it decided by a missed extra-point kick is like going to the ballet to see Baryshnikov trip.

Gene Klein, former Chargers owner
First Down and a Billion, 1987

It's a funny game, football, a sport in which guys 260 or 270 pounds club each other for fun and profit and then somebody not much bigger than a flamenco dancer comes bouncing onto the field to decide who wins or loses.

Art Spander, sports columnist
San Francisco Examiner, 1988

We like Ruben Rodriguez, even though he does occasionally kick one straight up in the air.

Mike McCormack, Seahawks
president, on his punter, 1988

I have two Christmas wishes. One is fifteen seconds in a dark alley to ask Buddy why he did it, and the other is fifteen seconds in a dark alley to beat the shit out of him.

Luis Zendejas, Cowboys placekicker,
after Eagles coach Buddy Ryan
allegedly offered a $200 "bounty" to
put Zendejas out of a game, 1989

🏈 SPORTSWRITERS

Often an All-American is made by a long run, a weak defense, and a poet in the press box.

Bob Zuppke, Illinois coach

Naw, man, journalism—it was easier.

Joe Namath, Jets quarterback, when
asked if he had majored in basket
weaving at Alabama, 1970

The great sportswriters think that if you're Shake Tiller you're supposed to be able to catch every flea that ever ran up a dog's ass.

Dan Jenkins,
sportswriter and novelist
Semi-Tough, 1972

Some people think I have to get down on all fours to eat my couple of pounds of raw meat a day. Others think that George Halas taught me to walk upright and I have an agent do my reading and writing for me. But people who really know me know that I can read a little. I move my lips sometimes, but I can read things on a second-grade level, like newspapers.

> Dick Butkus, Bears linebacker

A top editor of the *Dallas Morning News* once banned the use of nicknames like "Tommy," "Charlie," etc. A football writer promptly reported: "Doak Walker has been sidelined by a Charles horse."

> Larry Guest, *Orlando Sentinel*
> sportswriter

We'd have thirty seconds of respectful silence and then continue with enthusiasm.

> George Atkinson, Raiders cornerback,
> when asked what players would do if
> the press box blew up during a game,
> 1977

Pro football is the prestige beat, the biggest of them all, and sports editors almost never let a woman near it. . . . They think it's like sending a dog to do your income-tax return, or something.

> Betty Cuniberti,
> *Washington Post* sportswriter
> *The New Yorker*, 1979

I never read any stories about me. I already know about myself. I don't reckon they can tell me anything I don't know.

> Herschel Walker,
> Georgia running back, 1981

I'm sweating more answering your questions than I did in the game.

> Terry Bradshaw, Steelers
> quarterback, after a 34–7 loss, 1981

It was a brain transplant. I got a sportswriter's brain so I could be sure I had one that hadn't been used.

Norm Van Brocklin, former
quarterback and coach, when asked
about his operation, 1981

I don't want you writing anything nice about me. I might have to live up to it.

Woody Hayes, former Ohio State
coach, 1983

I've driven lots of automobiles, but I can't fix them. I've been to lots of hospitals, but I ain't no doctor. Are you telling me that when a guy who has never coached a game of professional football tells me I'm not coaching right, I'm not supposed to be upset?

Bum Phillips, Saints coach
Seattle Post-Intelligencer, 1984

The kid's got a warped mind. He wants to be a sportswriter.

Bo Schembechler, Michigan coach,
on his son
The Sporting News, 1985

Coaches appreciate media support, even though I know Bo Schembechler doesn't agree with you all the time. He told me if he walked across water, the headline on the story would be "Bo Schembechler Can't Swim."

Lou Holtz, University of Minnesota
coach
Chicago Sun-Times, 1985

I like sportswriters, really I do. I like 'em as much as I like referees.

Bo Schembechler, Michigan coach
Orange County Register, 1989

SUPER BOWL

If it's the ultimate, how come they're playing it again next year?

> Duane Thomas,
> Cowboys running back
> *Newsweek,* 1971

The Super Bowl is like Christmas shopping at Macy's for bookies.

> Larry Merchant, sportswriter
> *And Every Day You Take Another*
> *Bite,* 1971

More than being concerned with who's going to win the Super Bowl, I feel the Lord is probably more concerned that they might find a day other than Sunday to play it on.

> Billy Graham, evangelist

You can go to the bank and borrow money, but you can't go to the bank and borrow a Super Bowl ring. The ring is like a crown.

> "Mean Joe" Greene,
> Steelers defensive tackle, 1975

The Super Bowl is a week-long talk show. It's the event where reporters spend more time interviewing each other than they do talking to the athletes.

> Ira Miller, sportswriter
> *San Francisco Chronicle,* 1979

The score belongs on the society pages. To preserve the spirit of the occasion, the teams should have played in tuxes or swallowtail coats and corsages. It's not an athletic event anymore, it's a carnival. Mardi Gras with first downs.

> Jim Murray, sports columnist
> *Los Angeles Times,* 1980

Every year at this time I go to the Super Bowl and fail to cover it. I might as well try to cover Christmas.

Roy Blount, Jr., humorist
Esquire, 1980

I always wanted to win the Super Bowl so I could take it and hold it and see what lies beyond it. I think it may be the sun.

Peter Gent, former Cowboys receiver
Esquire, 1980

The Super Bowl has become more of a staging event for a week of debauchery than a contest to determine the best team in the National Football League.

Peter H. King, journalist
San Francisco Examiner, 1980

The Super Bowl is a kind of corporate Woodstock.

Michael Ruby, sportswriter
Inside Sports, 1981

Someone's going to win and someone's going to lose.

Ralph Nader, consumer advocate,
when asked his opinion
on the Super Bowl
San Francisco Examiner, 1981

The Super Bowl is a lot of sound and fury signifying nothing.

Robert Redford, actor
San Francisco Examiner, 1981

They want to be able to stage the Epic Game. They want it to be Army versus Carlisle. That way they can sell more T-shirts.

Bill Walsh, 49ers coach, 1981

The Super Bowl is a three-hour interruption in a week of drink and Rotarian parties.

> Roger Kahn, writer
> *Sport,* 1981

One of the great expense-account weeks of the year has ended, and the rest of the story will be written by accountants.

> Herb Caen, columnist
> *San Francisco Chronicle,* 1981

All those Super Bowls kind of blend in. The only reason they stand out in my memory is that we lost all of them.

> Alan Page, defensive tackle, on his
> four Super Bowls with the Vikings
> *San Francisco Examiner,* 1981

If Jesus were alive today, he would be at the Super Bowl.

> Norman Vincent Peale, evangelist
> *Time,* 1982

To love the Super Bowl, you only have to think what Januarys were like before it came along.

> David N. Rosenthal, journalist
> *Time,* 1982

Do you know anyone who's actually been to a Super Bowl? Of course not, unless your friends hobnob with the Fortune 500.

> Glen Waggoner, sportswriter
> *Sport,* 1983

It may end up in the gutter, but if it does, I'll be wearing it.

> Mark Moseley, Redskins placekicker,
> on his Super Bowl ring
> *Sports Illustrated,* 1983

To keep from walking around in circles for the rest of my life, I'll need another ring the same size on the other hand.

> John Riggins, Redskins running
> back, on his Super Bowl ring
> *The Sporting News*, 1983

Hell, a football game is a football game—that's the easy part. The most important thing for a coach to know about the Super Bowl is how to handle the hoopla.

> John Madden, former Raiders coach
> *Hey, Wait a Minute,*
> *I Wrote a Book!*, 1984

We honor winners in capitalism. No one is forgotten any faster than the loser of the Super Bowl.

> Brent Musburger, sportscaster
> *USA Today*, 1984

It's ridiculous for a country to get all worked up about a game—except the Super Bowl, of course. Now that's important.

> Andy Rooney, syndicated columnist,
> 1984

It has to be the worst title for any athletic event in the world. Nothing even comes close: Not the Bluebonnet Bowl football game or the Joe Garagiola–Tucson Open golf tournament or the Crackerjack Old-Timers Baseball Classic.

> John McGrath, sportswriter
> *Denver Post*, 1985

It's been my impression over the years as a passing viewer that the hype of the game is generally much better than the game itself.

> Linda Ellerbee, journalist
> *Sport*, 1987

You say, "If dying is it, I got to die here."

> L. C. Greenwood,
> Steelers defensive end
> *Denver Post,* 1987

The halftime show will look like a Moonie wedding at Madison Square Garden. Nine thousand clean-shaven Young Republicans will swarm the field, releasing nineteen thousand balloons, wearing yellow bib overalls, dancing with ninety-nine midgets who are wearing Rocky the Flying Squirrel costumes, while lip-synching Barry Manilow's remake of Steppenwolf's "Born to Be Wild."

> Mike Downey, sports columnist
> *Inside Sports,* 1987

SUPER BOWL I, 1967—PACKERS 35, CHIEFS 10

I haven't seen anything in the films that offers much of a threat to me. . . . I guarantee you they won't beat me on a deep pattern.

> Fred "The Hammer" Williamson,
> Chiefs cornerback, before Max
> McGee beat him for a thirty-seven-
> yard touchdown on the first play of
> the game, 1967

If I'd known it was going to be this big, I'd have kept the football.

> Max McGee, Packers receiver, on the
> Super Bowl
> *Time,* 1986

SUPER BOWL II, 1968—PACKERS 33, RAIDERS 14

You damn better well not let that Mickey Mouse league beat you. It'd be a disgrace, a complete, utter disgrace.

> Vince Lombardi, Packers coach, to
> his team, 1968

SUPER BOWL III, 1969—JETS 16, COLTS 7

The AFL is getting its share of truly competitive, gung-ho athletes, and it will soon achieve parity with the NFL. But that parity has not yet been reached, and the Colts should demonstrate this with an authority that may shock Jets fans.

> Tex Maule, football analyst
> *Sports Illustrated,* 1969

Damn, Joe, we better stop watching those movies or we're going to get overconfident.

> Pete Lammons, Jets fullback, to
> quarterback Joe Namath, 1969

We're going to win Sunday. I guarantee you.

> Joe Namath, at a dinner in Miami
> three days before the game, when the
> team was a seventeen-point
> underdog, 1969

Tiny Tim decked John Wayne Sunday.

> Dave Brady, sportswriter
> *The Washington Post,* 1969

After all the celebrating that went on, I don't think anybody was in any condition to think about things like who had the trophy. Some of the guys had enough trouble finding the airport.

> Frank Ramos, Jets public relations
> director, on the Jets leaving the
> Super Bowl trophy in Miami, 1969

SUPER BOWL VI, 1972—COWBOYS 24, DOLPHINS 3

I thought it was some idiot calling at that late hour.

> Don Shula, Dolphins coach, when
> President Richard M. Nixon called
> the night before the game
> with a play, 1972

God didn't want us to win the game because He wanted to make us better people.

> Bob Griese, Dolphins quarterback,
> 1972

SUPER BOWL VII, 1973—DOLPHINS 14, REDSKINS 7

We lost to the undefeated Miami team, but I held for extra points. I got to play in the Super Bowl. I got my knee dirty.

Sam Wyche,
former Redskins quarterback
Sports Illustrated, 1989

SUPER BOWL X, 1976—STEELERS 21, COWBOYS 17

I don't like this place. It's for people with arthritis. They come here to play golf and die.

Ernie Holmes, Steelers defensive
tackle, on Miami, 1976

SUPER BOWL XIII, 1979—STEELERS 35, COWBOYS 31

It's macho versus chivalry. Blood and guts versus head and heart. Snarls versus smiles.

Skip Bayless, Dallas sportswriter,
1979

Pittsburgh may have a little better team, but we've got two weeks to get ready. Give Tom Landry two weeks and he'd have beaten Nazi Germany.

Doug Todd, Cowboys publicist, 1979

SUPER BOWL XIV, 1980—STEELERS 31, RAMS 19

Reporter: Is your leg really broken?
Youngblood: No, I'm just pretending.

Jack Youngblood,
Rams defensive end, 1980

SUPER BOWL XV, 1981—RAIDERS 27, EAGLES 10

There are two teams in this year's Super Bowl, the good guys and the bad guys. We won't tell you who the bad guys are, but Oakland has never been called the "City of Brotherly Love."

Walter Cronkite, newscaster
"CBS Evening News," CBS-TV, 1981

Man, if I'm sleeping, how will I know what kind of good time somebody is having without me?

John Matuszak, Raiders defensive
end, hitting New Orleans the night
before the game, 1981

If he were on the Eagles, he'd be back on a plane to Philadelphia right now.

Dick Vermeil, Eagles coach, on
Matuszak, 1981

SUPER BOWL XVI, 1982—49ERS 26, BENGALS 21

The NFL has promised Detroit it could have the Super Bowl again, just as soon as it domes the entire city.

Scott Ostler, sports columnist
Los Angeles Times, 1982

SUPER BOWL XVII, 1983—REDSKINS 27, DOLPHINS 17

Imagine, thirty years from now people will be talking about that Super Bowl or this Super Bowl. I mean, if people thirty years from now even know what football *is*.

Bob Kuechenberg, Dolphins center,
1983

SUPER BOWL XVIII, 1984—RAIDERS 38, REDSKINS 9

I'm not talking to anybody today, 'cause if I talk today, I'll have nothing to say tomorrow.

John Riggins, Redskins running
back, to reporters, 1984

This will be NFL Films' answer to the "Texas Chainsaw Massacre."

> Steve Sabol, head of NFL Films, after
> the game, 1984
> *The Sporting News*, 1984

SUPER BOWL XX, 1986—BEARS 46, PATRIOTS 10

Reporter: Are you ready for Bourbon Street?
McMahon: The question is: Is Bourbon Street ready for me?

> Jim McMahon, Bears quarterback,
> 1986

Before the end, it kind of felt like we were the team that the Globetrotters play all the time.

> Ron Wooten, Patriots guard
> *Sports Illustrated*, 1986

SUPER BOWL XXI, 1987—GIANTS 39, BRONCOS 20

The Giants are in the Super Bowl. I haven't seen this much excitement in New York since they made shoplifting a misdemeanor.

> David Letterman
> "Late Night with David Letterman"
> NBC-TV, 1987

There were twenty-six hundred media people. . . . Multiply that number by the number of dumb and irrelevant questions each person has in them and you know you are likely to be playing King of the Hill on a pile of horseshit.

> Lawrence Taylor, Giants linebacker
> *LT: Living on the Edge*, 1987

SUPER BOWL XXIV, 1990—49ERS 55, BRONCOS 10

I see this as a *no más* situation. There is no way the 49ers can lose. It could be 55–3 by halftime.

> Terry Bradshaw, CBS-TV broadcaster
> *San Francisco Chronicle*, 1990

From the outset, the Broncos were not exactly a profile in courage. On the first play, quarterback John Elway threw too low. On the second, he threw too high. On the third, he ran for his life. Less than a minute into Super Bowl XXIV, it already was time for a Heimlich maneuver.

> Bernie Miklasz, sportswriter
> *St. Louis Post-Dispatch,* 1990

I'm sure the American workplace will be adversely affected on Monday, the day after XXIV. The game will be the focus of conversation . . . not to mention millions of hangovers. I wouldn't buy a toaster or a parachute manufactured the day after Super Bowl XXIV.

> Robert Klein, comedian
> *The New York Times,* 1990

 TELEVISION AND RADIO

Bell: Instead of saying the man fumbled the ball, say it escaped him.
Brickhouse: What was I supposed to say about the fight? Was I to have said they were having a Maypole dance?

> Jack Brickhouse, Bears broadcaster,
> to NFL commissioner Bert Bell

You'd stick that thing in a coffin.

> Vince Lombardi, Packers coach, to an
> interviewer who thrust a microphone
> in his face

Today the football games are a series of matchups to see who leads in blimp shots.

> Howard Cosell, sportscaster
> *Sports Illustrated,* 1967

Jayne Kennedy, CBS's gift to lobotomized sports fans. . . .
When Kennedy said at halftime she was surprised at the
Rams' lead, you had the impression she also was surprised
that no one had hit a home run.

> Howard Rosenberg,
> television columnist
> *Los Angeles Times*, 1980

If a football player ever whipped out a switchblade knife and
cut the throat of an opposing player, the announcer would
probably say, "Well, there's a little temper flare-up down
there."

> Mike Royko, columnist
> *Chicago Sun-Times*, 1981

After they break somebody's legs, you see the players turning toward the camera: "Hi, Mom!"

> Robert Klein, comedian
> "Robert Klein," HBO-TV, 1982

Every time [CBS-TV broadcaster] Phyllis George opens her
mouth, she sets the feminist movement back five years.

> Patrick Fuller, letter to the editor
> *San Francisco Chronicle*, 1982

Last week on a television show I said, "Some people don't
know a football from a banana." The next morning a local
banana distributor sent me a huge crate of bananas. This
week I'm going to say, "Some people don't know a football
from a Mercedes."

> John McKay, Buccaneers coach
> *Sport*, 1983

Pat Summerall has the most fluid delivery of any jock announcer. But with his paucity of speech and his understate-
ment, he's in danger of becoming a national cure for
insomnia.

> Howard Cosell, sportscaster
> *Inside Sports*, 1981

If I ever got cancer, I'd want Pat Summerall to be the one to tell me.

> Beano Cook, football analyst
> *Inside Sports*, 1987

He even cries at K-Mart openings.

> Frank Chirkinian, CBS-TV producer,
> on Summerall
> *Sports Illustrated*, 1987

Whenever we do the Thanksgiving game in Dallas and they play "The Battle Hymn of the Republic," he starts crying like a baby. That's America to Patrick—sitting in the Dallas booth with some good barbecue, a Dixie cup of foamy Coors, and "The Battle Hymn of the Republic."

> Tom Brookshier, television colleague,
> on Summerall
> *Inside Sports*, 1981

Brookie has only one wish in life: to run out of breath and money at the same time.

> Pat Summerall, on Brookshier
> *Inside Sports*, 1981

Pete Rozelle once said that only 1½ percent of the people watching TV football bet, and I said they all live on my block in New York.

> Beano Cook, football analyst
> *Inside Sports*, 1982

He's a jerk. . . . Charlie lost twelve times to the Vikings, and all of a sudden he's an expert on how to beat Minnesota.

> Gary Danielson, Lions quarterback,
> on former teammate Charlie Sanders,
> now a radio commentator
> *Seattle Post-Intelligencer*, 1984

I saw John Madden on TV, and the thought ran through my mind: How big would he be if he *didn't* drink Lite Beer.

> David Letterman,
> on the CBS-TV broadcast
> "Late Night with David Letterman,"
> NBC-TV, 1982

If it remains tied after two overtimes, the first team to name every product John Madden endorses wins.

> Tony Kornheiser, sportswriter
> *The Washington Post,* 1986

John is the one man who doesn't let success go to his clothes.

> Mike Ditka, Bears coach, on Madden
> *Sports Illustrated,* 1987

According to a recent survey, Jimmy the Greek, the sports analyst on CBS during the football season, gets more fake telephone numbers from women than any other man alive.

> David Letterman
> "Late Night with David Letterman,"
> NBC-TV, 1987

He was no better at forecasting than most Holiday Inn bartenders.

> Terri Frei, sportscaster,
> on Jimmy the Greek
> *The Oregonian,* 1988

Seven minutes? That's how long the replay judge deliberated over a decision in Sunday's game. Seven minutes to look at a TV replay? What does the man do for a living? Unload baggage from airplanes at LAX?

> Scott Ostler, sports columnist
> *Los Angeles Times,* 1986

I thought they [the officials] were ordering a pizza.

> Neil Lomax, Cardinals quarterback,
> on a long replay delay
> *Sports Illustrated,* 1986

He's a real child of the media. If you put a stethoscope to his heart you'd probably hear jingles from famous commercials.

> Ahmad Rashad, on fellow NBC-TV
> broadcaster Bob Costas
> *Rashad,* 1988

I know Keith Jackson is a cornball, but he brings more personality to a football game than all the other vanilla voices combined. When I hear Jackson talking about linemen "swapping paint in the trenches" I *know* I'm at a college football game.

> Tom Gilmore, sportswriter,
> on ABC-TV's broadcaster
> *San Francisco Chronicle,* 1990

 **TRAINING CAMP**

To break training camp without permission is an act of treason.

> John W. Heisman,
> Pennsylvania coach
> *Principles of Football,* 1921

I need more time for beer drinking and dating.

> Frank Sinkwich, Georgia running
> back, quitting spring practice, 1941

All I know is that we went out there in two buses and came back in one.

> Gene Stallings, Texas A&M defensive
> end, when asked if practice had been
> tough, 1966

Nothing happens in football training camps except some shoulder separations.

Leonard Shecter, sportswriter
The Jocks, 1970

You can't really tell anything from spring practice. It's like having your daughter come in at four o'clock in the morning with a Gideons Bible.

Dan Fambrough, Kansas coach

You won't believe this, but the hardest part of every training camp for me is starting to wear a helmet again. The first time I put it on, my head goes "clunk!" over to one side.

Norm Evans,
Dolphins offensive tackle
The Miami Herald, 1973

The heat is entirely mental. When you pass out, it becomes physical.

Tom Landry, Cowboys coach

You'll do anything to break the routine. One night I sneaked out of camp at 1:30 A.M. and drove as fast as I could seventeen and a half miles just to get one beer. One beer. A thirty-four-mile round trip, speeding, breaking curfew, sneaking back into the dormitory. For one lousy beer. And I hate beer. But that's what training camp drives you to do.

Alex Karras,
former Lions defensive tackle
The Miami Herald, 1973

Training camp is not my natural habitat.

Bob Griese, Dolphins quarterback

Training camp is like kissing an ugly girl. At first there's fear of the unknown, but once you get started it's not so bad.

Dave Casper, Raiders tight end

I love training camp because that's the only time of the season I get to play.

Bill Bain, Rams guard

God made football just so water would taste good.

Derland Moore, Saints defensive
tackle
San Jose Mercury News, 1979

I never scrimmage Oilers against Oilers. . . . What for? Houston isn't on our schedule.

Bum Phillips, Oilers coach
He Ain't No Bum, 1979

If God wanted it so hot, why did He invent people?

Claude Humphrey,
Eagles defensive end
Sports Illustrated, 1980

I'd like to know why people are interested in my nightlife. It's no different than anybody else's during training camp. Most evenings I'll just swing by the Christian Science reading room, pick up a good book, then swing by the Burger King and get some chow. After that I just head back to the dorm where I can kick back and read.

Ken Stabler, Oilers quarterback
Sports Illustrated, 1980

I also have to get my first-day walk mastered. This is the same walk that every veteran player uses when he arrives in camp. It says: Look, I'm in great shape. And it's a terrific walk, but it takes some practice to get it straight.

Ahmad Rashad, Vikings receiver
Sports Illustrated, 1982

I like training camp because I'm not married and I don't have anybody to cook for me. No more hamburgers for at least four weeks.

Rich Karlis, Broncos placekicker
The Sporting News, 1983

The only reason I played baseball at all in college was to get out of spring football.

> Tom Paciorek, Chicago White Sox
> infielder and former Houston
> University linebacker

The highlight was when Alan Zendejas, a placekicker from Arizona State, fainted during his blood test.

> John Elliott, Michigan offensive
> tackle, on the NFL scouting camp,
> 1988

 **WIN, LOSE, AND TIE**

Winning is not everything. It is the only thing.

> Fielding Yost, Michigan coach, 1905

All quitters are good losers.

> Bob Zuppke, Illinois coach

One loss is good for the soul. Too many losses are not good for the coach.

> Knute Rockne, Notre Dame coach

I'm a win man myself. I don't go for place or show.

> Bear Bryant, Kentucky coach, 1950

The only thing worse than finishing second is to be lying on the desert alone with your back broken. Either way, nobody ever finds out about you.

> Red Sanders, UCLA coach, 1954

When you win, you're an old pro. When you lose, you're an old man.

> Charley Cornerly,
> former Giants quarterback

When you're playing for the national championship, it's not a matter of life and death. It's more important than that.

> Duffy Daugherty,
> Michigan State coach, 1965

A missed block here, a missed assignment there, it adds up.

> Joe Kuharich, Eagles coach, after
> losing 56–7 to the Cowboys, 1966

I know all about opening victories. My first season we started out 1 and 0 and ended up 1 and 13.

> Chuck Noll, Steelers coach, on the
> 1969 season, 1972

You can take your wars and your starvation and your fires and your floods, but there's no heartbreak in life like losing the big game in high school.

> Dan Jenkins,
> sportswriter and novelist
> *Semi-Tough,* 1972

When you're 2–8, you don't mess around with any unsigned fruitcake.

> Less Corso, Indiana coach, when he
> received a fruitcake in the mail, 1973

Without winners there wouldn't be any goddamned civilization.

> Woody Hayes, Ohio State coach, 1974

■ ■ ■

When you're winning, you don't need any friends. When you're losing, you don't have any friends anyway.

> Woody Hayes

Reporter: What about the Bucs' execution?
McKay: I'm in favor of it.

> John McKay, Buccaneers coach,
> when his team had lost twenty-six
> straight, 1977

There's only one bright side of losing—the phone doesn't
ring as much the following week.

> Lou Holtz, Arkansas coach

Our offense wasn't very good. Our defense wasn't very good.
Our kicking game wasn't any good. And the coaching was
poor. When you have those four things going against you
and you only get beat by seven points, it's a miracle.

> Bo Schembechler, Michigan coach,
> after losing 21–14 to Wisconsin,
> 1981

You'd think we'd have won one just by accident.

> Tom Landry, Cowboys coach, after
> losing three straight NFC
> Championship games, 1982

Winning is a matter of opinion. But losing is a cold reality.

> Peter Gent, former Cowboys receiver

It's like the fish that got away. Is it to the fish's credit or is
it the fisherman's fault?

> Tim Tierney, Hayward State coach,
> after a tough loss
> *San Francisco Chronicle*, 1984

Losing makes you learn something, but I don't want to be
the smartest guy in the world.

> Bill Davis,
> South Carolina State coach
> *Seattle Post-Intelligencer*, 1984

All there is in life is winning. . . . Well, yeah, I suppose there are other things in life, but who cares?

Al Davis, Raiders managing general
partner, 1984

Whenever you do something, you got to win. I don't care if you and another kid are standing there seeing how far you can pee—*you* got to pee farther than the other guy.

Henry Lawrence,
Raiders offensive tackle

I don't know what happened. I was too busy having the worst game of my life.

Randy Cross, 49ers guard, after a
26–10 loss to the Bears
USA Today, 1985

Now I know how Custer felt at the Little Big Horn.

Stan Parrish, Kansas State coach,
after losing 56–10 to Oklahoma
USA Today, 1986

You're not going to win every game, but I hate to prove it right off the bat.

Jerry Burns, Vikings coach,
losing his debut
The Sporting News, 1986

We never got a ring for winning. We got a $9 blue blanket that said, "World Champions."

Bobby Layne, former Lions
quarterback, on winning the 1952
NFL title
The Sporting News, 1986

Isn't it funny how a win can warm you up? They don't look as cold on that side of the field as they do on this side.

John Madden, broadcaster, as the
Eagles led the Giants in
zero-degree weather
"NFL Football," CBS-TV, 1989

■ ■ ■

A tie is like kissing your sister.

> Allie Sherman, Giants coach, after his
> team tied the Cowboys 13–13
> *Esquire,* 1965

The alumni are always with you, win or tie.

> Duffy Daugherty,
> Michigan State coach, 1965

Come on, sissies. You gonna quit?

> Bubba Smith, Michigan State
> defensive end, when Notre Dame ran
> out the clock to settle for a 10–10 tie,
> 1966

I have a lot of seniors on this team. Some of them will be
graduating and going on over to Vietnam, I suppose. When
they get there, I just hope they don't play for a tie.

> Bear Bryant, Alabama coach, on
> Notre Dame's tie, 1966

What the Fighting Irish did was, they tied one for the Gipper.

> Dan Jenkins, sportswriter
> *Saturday's America,* 1970

I would have rather played all day and all night to settle the
game. Ties are what men get at Christmas and never wear.

> John McKay, Southern California
> coach on a 1968 tie with Notre Dame
> *McKay: A Coach's Story,* 1975

They say a tie is like kissing your sister. Well, I have three
beautiful sisters, and I kiss them all the time.

> Joe Kapp, California coach, after
> rallying to tie Arizona
> *Sports Illustrated,* 1983

"A tie is like kissing your sister"—except if your last name is Bissett.

> Glenn Sheeley, sportswriter, on
> actress Jacqueline Bissett
> *Inside Sports,* 1983

This tie is like kissing your brother. It tastes awful.

> Brian Bosworth, Oklahoma
> linebacker, after tying Texas 15–15
> *Seattle Post-Intelligencer,* 1984

 **WOMEN**

Clara Bow is off-limits to all members of this football team.

> Joe Morella, Southern California
> coach, after the "It Girl" invited team
> members to her Hollywood mansion,
> 1927

The only time we're together is when somebody is taking our picture.

> Yvonne Ameche, wife of Wisconsin
> running back Alan, 1954

I know I'm not very pretty, but then the girls I talk to aren't very pretty either. Even with them I can't make out. I couldn't make out if I had the Hope Diamond hanging from my neck.

> Alex Karras, Lions defensive tackle,
> 1964

If you find a gal worth $1,000, call me, too. I'd like to see her myself.

> Vince Lombardi, Packers coach,
> threatening receiver Max McGee
> with a fine if he broke curfew again

I would rather score a touchdown on a particular day than make love to the prettiest girl in the United States.

> Paul Hornung, Packers running back
> *Football and the Single Man,* 1965

If things didn't work out, I didn't want to blow the whole day.

> Paul Hornung, on why he got
> married in the morning
> *Sports Illustrated,* 1967

I can't fool my wife at all. I just get red in the face. Jackie reads me better than I can read those linemen.

> Ray Nitschke, Packers linebacker,
> 1967

I call my girlfriend Will Rogers 'cause she never met a man she didn't like.

> Tommy Joe Crutcher, Packers
> linebacker, 1967

There is no place for women in football because to play football you need a bull neck, and I don't like women with bull necks.

> Woody Hayes, Ohio State coach

Divorce, no. Murder, yes.

> Anne Hayes, wife of Woody,
> when asked if she ever
> contemplated divorce

I'd like to tell you about what was actually the finest performance of my rookie season, but, shoot, I promised her I wouldn't.

> Joe Namath, Jets quarterback
> *I Can't Wait Until Tomorrow . . . ,*
> 1969

Some guys are born to be business tycoons or painters or something, but me, I was born to play football. I'll tell you, Fran, just between you and me, I'd rather play football than screw.

> Matt Hazeltine, Giants linebacker, to
> quarterback Fran Tarkenton, 1970

I don't like anybody very much except my wife, and some days I don't speak to *her*.

> Cornell Green, Cowboys cornerback,
> 1972

All she looks for is whether I get up.

> Dave Herman, Jets guard, when
> asked whether his wife watches
> him play

I've known women who thought football was worthless and brutal. But they don't understand the sport, and they don't understand the nature of the male.

> Paul Brown, Bengals coach, 1977

As far as cooking goes, the only time I expect a seven-course dinner is when I hand a girl seven cans and an opener.

> Ken Stabler, Raiders quarterback
> *Inside Sports*, 1980

You ought to take them TV dinners out of the boxes before you put 'em in the micro.

> Ken Stabler, advising his girlfriend,
> Wonderfully Wicked Wanda

I never solicit advice from my wife, Helen. . . . I don't help her cook, and she don't help me coach.

> Bum Phillips, Oilers coach
> *He Ain't No Bum*, 1979

I take my wife everywhere with me because she's too ugly
to kiss good-bye.

> Bum Phillips
> *He Ain't No Bum,* 1979

I think women belong in the kitchen.

> Edward DeBartolo, Jr., 49ers owner,
> banning female reporters from the
> locker room
> *San Jose Mercury News,* 1981

My father has always said that there were two things that
women, however brilliant, fail with great charm to understand: one is the International Date Line, the other is third
and ten.

> George Plimpton, writer and editor
> *Sports Illustrated,* 1981

After three or four days with a beautiful woman, it's time for
me to get going.

> John Matuszak,
> Raiders defensive end
> *Sport,* 1981

I once had a woman try to run me over in training camp. I
think that's bad for you.

> John Matuszak
> *Playboy,* 1981

I won't put my arm around a player. It's just not me. I'm
not a close person to anybody, not even my wife.

> Frank Kush, Colts coach
> *Inside Sports,* 1982

Hollywood made a movie of my life. The film had me pro-
posing to my wife on the football field. I would never misuse
a football field that way.

> Elroy "Crazy Legs" Hirsch, former
> Rams receiver
> *San Francisco Chronicle,* 1983

I had done all the work around the house, and my wife gave me two options—clean the toilets or clean behind the refrigerator. I thought it was time for me to get back to work.

> R. C. Thielemann, Falcons guard,
> ending a five-week holdout
> *The Sporting News*, 1983

That was the best friend I ever had. That car lasted longer than any girlfriend I've ever had.

> Harvey Martin, Cowboys defensive
> end, after he wrecked his new
> Mercedes-Benz
> *The Sporting News*, 1983

Actually, Sherrard was a stroll-on. He strolled onto campus with a girl on each arm. The kid was skin and bones, he had girls hanging all over him, and he told us he thought he could play football for UCLA.

> Homer Smith, UCLA offensive
> coordinator, on split end
> Mike Sherrard
> *Sports Illustrated*, 1983

Only three things scare me: tornadoes, wild women, and fumbles.

> Bill Parcells, Giants coach
> *Seattle Post-Intelligencer*, 1984

I don't know. I don't see her that much.

> Ray Perkins, Alabama coach, when
> asked if his wife resented his
> eighteen-hour workdays
> *Sports Illustrated*, 1984

Dump McKinney held one pro football record that would never be touched: He married three flight attendants and two Dallas Cowboy Cheerleaders.

> Dan Jenkins,
> sportswriter and novelist
> *Life Its Ownself*, 1984

She reminds me that *Playboy* is a lot like *National Geographic*. Both have pictures of places I'm never going to visit.

Don James, University of Washington
coach, on his wife

My wife looked at me and said, "Boy, you are skinny, aren't you." I said, "Honey, I'd like to remind you that it was minor defects like that that kept me from getting a better wife."

Lou Holtz, University of Minnesota
coach, 1984

We can't drink and we can't smoke and we can't chase women. Well, we can chase women, but we aren't allowed to catch them.

Glen Kozlowski, receiver, on life at
Brigham Young
The Sporting News, 1985

Believe it or not, where I come from I'm good-looking.

Mark Traynowicz, Bills rookie center
from Nebraska, on becoming
engaged to a former Miss Nebraska
The Sporting News, 1985

I've dated girls who were far better looking than the quality of girls who should be going out with me.

Cris Collinsworth, Bengals receiver,
on the benefits of playing in the
NFL, 1985

She's a fine-looking woman. 'Course, I wouldn't have married any other kind.

Bum Phillips, former coach,
on wife Helen
Los Angeles Times, 1986

The only place I ever went was a football game. And now he don't even take me there.

> Helen Phillips,
> on her husband's retirement
> *Los Angeles Times,* 1986

I run everything, but at home I'm second string.

> Bo Schembechler, Michigan coach
> "College Football," CBS-TV, 1986

Max ought to be in the Hall of Fame himself. He's fifty-six years old, and his wife's pregnant.

> Paul Hornung, former Packers
> running back on former teammate
> Max McGee
> *The Sporting News,* 1986

I wasn't looking for a starting quarterback. But I wasn't looking for a wife when I found one, either.

> Lou Holtz, Notre Dame coach,
> on Tony Rice
> *Sports Illustrated,* 1987

We had to separate Wives Day and Girlfriends Day. A couple of guys brought both.

> Jerry Glanville, Oilers coach
> *Sports Illustrated,* 1989

 **BIBLIOGRAPHY**

Allen, George. *Merry Christmas—You're Fired.* New York: Simon and Schuster, 1982.

———, and Mickey Herskowitz. *Motivation George Allen Style.* New York: McGraw-Hill, 1986.

Alzado, Lyle, with Paul Zimmerman. *Mile High: The Story of Lyle Alzado and the Amazing Denver Broncos.* New York: Berkley, 1978.

Anderson, Ken, with Jack Clary. *The Art of Quarterbacking.* New York: Linden Press, 1984.

Blount, Roy, Jr. *About Three Bricks Shy of a Load.* Boston: Little, Brown, 1974.

Bortstein, Larry. *Super Joe: The Joe Namath Story.* New York: Grosset & Dunlap, 1969.

Bosworth, Brian, with Rick Reilly. *The Boz: Confessions of a Modern Anti-Hero.* New York: Putnam, 1988.

Bradshaw, Terry, with Buddy Martin. *Looking Deep.* Chicago: Contemporary Books, 1989.

Brodie, John, and James D. Houston, *Open Field.* Boston: Houghton Mifflin, 1974.

Brondfield, Jerry. *Rockne: The Coach, The Man, The Legend.* New York: Random House, 1976.

———. *Woody Hayes and the 100-Yard War.* New York: Random House, 1974.

Brown, Jim, with Steve Delsohn. *Out of Bounds.* New York: Zebra Books, 1989.

Brown, Paul, with Jack Clary. *PB: The Paul Brown Story.* New York: Signet Books, 1986.

Bryant, Paul W., and John Underwood. *Bear: The Hard Life and Good Times of Alabama's Coach Bryant.* Boston: Little, Brown, 1976.

Butkus, Dick, and Robert W. Billings. *Stop-Action.* New York: E. P. Dutton, 1972.

Carson, Harry, and Joe Smith. *Point of Attack: A Season with the New York Giants.* New York: McGraw-Hill, 1986.

Chandler, Bob. *Violent Sundays.* New York: Simon and Schuster, 1984.

Clary, Jack. *Washington Redskins*. New York: Macmillan, 1974.
Cosell, Howard, with Peter Bonventre. *I Never Played the Game*. New York: William Morrow, 1985.
Curran, Bob. *The $400,000 Quarterback*. New York: Macmillan, 1965.
Curtis, Mike, with Bill Gilbert. *Keep Off My Turf*. Philadelphia: J. B. Lippincott, 1972.
Ditka, Mike, and Don Pierson. *Ditka: An Autobiography*. Chicago: Bonus Books, 1987.
Dobler, Conrad, and Vic Carucci. *They Call Me Dirty*. New York: Putnam, 1988.
Donovan, Arthur J., Jr., with Bob Drury. *Fatso: The Football Follies of Artie Donovan*. New York: William Morrow, 1987.
Dorsett, Tony, and Harvey Frommer. *Running Tough: Memories of a Football Maverick*. Garden City, NY: Doubleday, 1989.
Durant, John, and Lee Etter. *Highlights of College Football*. New York: Hastings House, 1970.
Evans, Norm, with Edwin Pope. *On the Line*. Old Tappan, NJ: Fleming H. Revell, 1976.
Fox, Larry. *Bert Jones and the Battling Colts*. New York: Dodd, Mead, 1977.
———. *Broadway Joe and His Super Jets*. New York: Coward-McCann, 1969.
———. *Mean Joe Greene and the Steelers' Front Four*. New York: Dodd, Mead, 1975.
Gent, Peter. *The Franchise*. New York: Villard Books, 1983.
———. *North Dallas Forty*. New York: William Morrow, 1973.
———. *North Dallas After Forty*. New York: Villard Books, 1989.
Gluck, Herb. *While the Gettin's Good: Inside the World Football League*. New York: Bobbs-Merrill, 1975.
Halas, George S., with Gwen Morgan and Arthur Veysey. *Halas: An Autobiography*. Chicago: Bonus Books, 1986.
Harrington, Denis. *Riggins in Motion*. New York: Pinnacle Books, 1985.
Harris, David. *The League: The Rise and Fall of the NFL*. New York: Bantam, 1986.
Hawkins, Alex. *My Story (And I'm Sticking to It)*. Chapel Hill, NC: Algonquin Books, 1989.
Henderson, Thomas, and Peter Knobler. *Out of Control: Confessions of an NFL Casualty*. New York: Putnam, 1987.
Herskowitz, Mickey. *The Legend of Bear Bryant*. New York: McGraw-Hill, 1988.
Holtz, Lou, with John Heisler. *The Fighting Spirit: A Championship Season at Notre Dame*. New York: Pocket Books, 1989.
Hyman, Mervin D., and Gordon S. White. *Big Ten Football*. New York: Macmillan, 1977.
Ignatin, George, and Allen Barra. *Football by the Numbers*. New York: Prentice-Hall, 1986.

Ioos, Walter, and Dan Jenkins. *Football.* New York: Abrams, 1986.
Jenkins, Dan. *Life Its Ownself.* New York: Simon and Schuster, 1984.
———. *Saturday's America.* Boston: Little, Brown, 1970.
———. *Semi-Tough.* New York: Atheneum, 1972.
Jones, Joey. *In Good Hands.* Huntsville, AL: Albright & Co., 1986.
Karras, Alex, with Herb Gluck. *Even Big Guys Cry.* New York: Holt, Rinehart and Winston, 1977.
Kaye, Ivan N., *Good Clean Violence: A History of College Football.* New York: J. B. Lippincott, 1973.
Kirby, James. *Fumble: Bear Bryant, Wally Butts and the Great College Football Scandal.* New York: Harcourt Brace Jovanovich, 1986.
Klecko, Joe, Fields, Joe, and Greg Logan. *Nose to Nose: Survival in the Trenches of the NFL.* New York: William Morrow, 1989.
Klein, Gene, and David Fisher. *First Down and a Billion: The Funny Business of Pro Football.* New York: William Morrow, 1987.
Knox, Chuck. *Hard Knox: The Life of an NFL Coach.* New York: Harcourt Brace Jovanovich, 1988.
Kopay, David, and Perry Deane Young. *The David Kopay Story.* New York: Arbor House, 1977.
Kramer, Jerry. Edited by Dick Schaap. *Farewell to Football.* New York: World Publishing, 1969.
———. *Instant Replay: The Green Bay Diary of Jerry Kramer.* New York: World Publishing, 1968.
Kramer, Jerry, with Dick Schaap. *Distant Replay: The Stars of the Green Bay Packers.* New York: Putnam, 1985.
Lamb, Kevin, and Terry Bannon. *Bearin' Down: A Celebration of the 1984 Chicago Bears.* Chicago: Contemporary Books, 1984.
Libby, Bill. *O.J.: The Story of Football's Fabulous O. J. Simpson.* New York: Putnam, 1974.
Lomax, Neil. *Third and Long.* New York: Fleming H. Revell, 1986.
Madden, John, with Dave Anderson. *Hey, Wait a Minute, I Wrote a Book!* New York: Villard Books, 1984.
———. *One Knee Equals Two Feet (And Everything Else You Need to Know About Football).* New York: Villard Books, 1986.
———. *One Size Doesn't Fit All.* New York: Villard Books, 1988.
Mandell, Arnold J. *The Nightmare Season.* New York: Random House, 1976.
Martin, Harvey. *Texas Thunder: My Eleven Years with the Dallas Cowboys.* New York: Rawson, 1986.
Matuszak, John, with Steve Delsohn. *Cruisin' with the Tooz.* New York: Franklin Watts, 1987.
McCallum, John D. *Pac-Ten Football.* Seattle, WA: Writing Works, 1982.
———, and Paul Castner. *We Remember Rockne.* Huntington, IN: Our Sunday Visitor, 1975.

McDonough, John, with Paul T. Owens. *Don't Hit Him, He's Dead*. Millbrae, CA: Celestial Arts, 1978.

McKay, John, with Jim Perry. *McKay: A Coach's Story*. New York: Atheneum, 1975.

McMahon, Jim, with Bob Verdi. *McMahon: The Bare Truth About Chicago's Brashest Bear*. New York: Warner Books, 1986.

Meggysey, Dave. *Out of Their League*. Palo Alto, CA: Ramparts, 1970.

Merchant, Larry. *And Every Day You Take Another Bite*. Garden City, NY: Doubleday, 1971.

Michelson, Herb, and Dave Newhouse. *Rose Bowl Football Since 1902*. New York: Stein and Day, 1977.

Montana, Joe, and Bob Raissman. *Audibles: My Life in Football*. New York: William Morrow, 1986.

———, and Alan Steinberg. *Cool Under Fire: Reflections on the San Francisco 49ers*. Boston: Little, Brown, 1989.

Moody, Fred. *Fighting Chance: An NFL Season with the Seattle Seahawks*. Seattle, WA: Sasquatch Books, 1989.

Morris, Jeannie. *Brian Piccolo: A Short Season*. New York: Rand McNally, 1971.

Namath, Joe Willie, with Dick Schaap. *I Can't Wait Until Tomorrow: 'Cause I Get Better-Looking Every Day*. New York: Random House, 1969.

Nash, Bruce, and Allan Zullo. *The Football Hall of Shame*. New York: Pocket Books, 1986.

Nelson, Mark, and Mark Bonner. *The Semi-Official Dallas Cowboys Haters' Handbook*. New York: Collier Books, 1984.

Newsom, Ted, and John D. Brancato. *The Unofficial NFL Players Handbook*. New York: Simon and Schuster, 1984.

Nitschke, Ray, with Robert W. Wells. *Mean on Sunday: The Autobiography of Ray Nitschke*. Garden City, NY: Doubleday, 1973.

Olderman, Murray. *Super!* Los Angeles, CA: Los Angeles Raiders/Murray Olderman, 1984.

Oliver, Chip. Edited by Ron Rapoport. *High for the Game*. New York: William Morrow, 1971.

Oriad, Michael. *The End of Autumn: Reflections on My Life in Football*. Garden City, NY: Doubleday, 1982.

Paige, Woodrow, Jr. *Orange Madness: The Incredible Odyssey of the Denver Broncos*. New York: Thomas Y. Crowell, 1978.

Parrish, Bernie. *The Call It a Game*. New York: Dial Press, 1971.

Paul, William Henry. *The Gray-Flannel Pigskin: Movers and Shakers of Pro Football*. Philadelphia: J. B. Lippincott, 1974.

Perkins, Steve. *The Dallas Cowboys: Winning the Big One*. New York: Grosset & Dunlap, 1972.

Phillips, O. A. "Bum," and Ray Buck. *He Ain't No Bum*. New York: Jordan & Co., 1979.

Plimpton, George. *Mad Ducks and Bears*. New York: Random House, 1973.
———. *Paper Lion*. New York: Harper & Row, 1965.
———, with Bill Curry. *One More July*. New York: Harper & Row, 1977.
Plunkett, Jim, and Dave Newhouse. *The Jim Plunkett Story*. New York: Arbor House, 1981.
Pope, Edwin. *Football's Greatest Coaches*. Atlanta, GA: Tupper and Love, 1955.
Prugh, Jeff. *The Herschel Walker Story*. New York: Ballantine, 1983.
Rashad, Ahmad, with Peter Bodo. *Rashad*. New York: Viking, 1988.
Riggins, John, and Jack Winter. *Gameplan: The Language and Strategy of Pro Football*. Santa Barbara, CA: Santa Barbara Press, 1984.
Rockne, Dick. *Bow Down to Washington: A Story of Husky Football*. Huntsville, AL: Strode Publishers, 1975.
Rockne, Knute K. *Coaching*. New York: AMS Press, 1925.
Rodgers, Pepper. *Fourth and Long Gone*. Atlanta, GA: Peachtree Publishers, 1984.
Rosenthal, Harold. *Fifty Faces of Football*. New York: Atheneum, 1981.
Sahadi, Lou. *The Long Pass*. New York: World Publishing, 1974.
Sayers, Gale, with Al Silverman. *I Am Third*. New York: Viking, 1970.
Schembechler, Bo, and Mitch Albom. *Bo*. New York: Warner Books, 1989.
Schoor, Gene. *Football's Greatest Coach: Vince Lombardi*. Garden City, NY: Doubleday, 1974.
Shaw, Gary. *Meat on the Hoof: The Hidden World of Texas Football*. New York: St. Martin's, 1972.
Shula, Don, with Lou Sahadi. *The Winning Edge*. New York: E. P. Dutton, 1973.
Singletary, Mike, with Armen Keteyian. *Calling the Shots: Inside the Chicago Bears*. Chicago: Contemporary Books, 1986.
Stabler, Ken, and Barry Stainback. *Snake*. New York: Doubleday, 1986.
———, with Dick O'Connor. *Super Bowl Diary: The Autobiography of Ken "The Snake" Stabler*. New York: Pinnacle Books, 1977.
Staubach, Roger, with Sam Blair and Bob St. John. *First Down, Lifetime to Go*. Waco, TX: Word Books, 1974.
Steele, Michael R. *Knute Rockne: A Bio-Bibliography*. Westport, CT: Greenwood Press, 1986.
Stingley, Darryl, with Mark Mulvoy. *Happy to Be Alive*. New York: Beaufort Books, 1983.
Stowers, Carlton. *Journey to Triumph: 110 Dallas Cowboys Tell Their Stories*. Dallas, TX: Taylor Publishing, 1982.

Stram, Hank, with Lou Sahadi. *They're Playing My Game.* New York: William Morrow, 1986.

Sullivan, George. *The Great Running Backs.* New York: Putnam, 1972.

Tarkenton, Fran, and Jack Olson. *Better Scramble Than Lose.* New York: Four Winds Press, 1969.

———, with Herb Resnicow. *Murder at the Super Bowl.* New York: William Morrow, 1986.

———, with Brock Yates. *Broken Patterns: The Education of a Quarterback.* New York: Simon and Schuster, 1971.

Tatum, Jack. *They Call Me Assassin.* New York: Everest House, 1979.

Taylor, Lawrence, and David Falkner. *LT: Living on the Edge.* New York: Times Books, 1987.

Thorn, John, ed., with David Reuther. *The Armchair Quarterback.* New York: Charles Scribner's Sons, 1982.

Tips, Kern. *Football—Texas Style: An Illustrated History of the Southwest Conference.* Garden City, NY: Doubleday, 1964.

Tittle, Y. A. *Y. A. Tittle: I Pass!* New York: Franklin Watts, 1964.

Toomay, Pat. *The Crunch.* New York: W. W. Norton, 1975.

———. *On Any Given Sunday.* New York: Donald I. Fine, 1984.

Twombly, Wells. *Blanda: Alive and Kicking.* Los Angeles, CA: Nash Publishing, 1972.

———. *Shake Down the Thunder!: The Official Biography of Notre Dame's Frank Leahy.* Radnor, PA: Chilton Book Co., 1974.

Underwood, John. *The Death of an American Game: The Crisis in Football.* Boston: Little, Brown, 1979.

Weyand, Alexander M. *Football Immortals.* New York: Macmillan, 1962.

Whittingham, Richard. *What a Game They Played.* New York: Harper & Row, 1984.

Whittingham, Richard, ed. *The Fireside Book of Pro Football.* New York: Simon & Schuster, 1989.

Whittingham, Richard. *The Chicago Bears.* New York: Simon and Schuster, 1986.

Youngblood, Jack, with Joel Engel. *Blood.* Chicago: Contemporary Books, 1988.

Zimmerman, Paul. *The New Thinking Man's Guide to Pro Football.* New York: Simon and Schuster, 1984.

INDEX

Adamle, Mike, 29
Adams, Bud, 139
Afflis, Dick, 155
Agase, Alex, 31, 203
Akers, Fred, 37, 204
Alborn, Ray, 32, 66, 205
Albrecht, Ted, 80
Alexander, Willie, 207
Ali, Muhammad, 84
Allen, Byron, 67
Allen, George, 39, 40, 41, 45,
   101, 135
Allen, George E., 38
Allen, Marcus, 55, 212
Allen, Maury, 198
Alzado, Lyle, 18, 75, 121, 122,
   123, 158, 162
Ameche, Alan, 248
Ameche, Yvonne, 248
Anderson, Dave, 146
Anderson, Gary, 211
Andrews, William, 195
Antak, Al, 222
Applebome, Peter, 133
Ashe, Arthur, 138
Atkins, Doug, 43, 76
Atkinson, George, 225
Avedisian, Charley, 190
Axthelm, Pete, 60, 122, 199

Babitz, Eve, 102
Bacon, Coy, 76, 153
Baer, Bugs, 151
Bailey, Sam, 152
Bain, Bill, 155, 242
Baird, Bill, 72
Baker, Russell, 114, 184
Bakken, Jim, 158
Bankhead, Tallulah, 96
Barger, Sonny, 163
Barnes, Billy, 146
Barnidge, Tom, 12
Barra, Allen, 56, 197
Bartkowski, Steve, 181
Baryshnikov, Mikhail, 223

Bass, Dick, 82
Bates, Billy, 220
Battle, Mike, 73, 221
Baugh, Sammy, 190
Bayless, Skip, 68, 137, 233
Bell, Bert, 236
Bender, Gary, 18
Bennett, Ben, 58
Bennett, Leeman, 132
Berkow, Ira, 103
Berle, Milton, 143
Bestwick, Dick, 152
Bethea, Elvin, 76
Betters, Doug, 118
Bicknell, Jack, 12
Bidwell, Charles "Stormy," 162
Biletnikoff, Fred, 131
Bingaman, Les, 76
Birdwell, Dan, 76
Birdwell, Diane, 76
Bisher, Furman, 141, 164, 201
Blaik, Red, 180
Blanchard, Doc, 210
Blanda, George, 34, 160
Bleier, Rocky, 211, 212
Blount, Mel, 72
Blount, Roy, Jr., 228
Bokamper, Kim, 118
Bolton, Ron, 15, 73
Bombeck, Erma, 13
Boone, Pat, 36
Boswell, Thomas, 31
Bosworth, Brian, 44, 70, 118,
   119, 192, 196, 248
Bosworth, Kathy, 119
Bouton, Jim, 127
Bow, Clara, 248
Bowden, Bobby, 23, 53, 160
Boyarksy, Jerry, 75, 77
Braase, Ordell, 166
Bradley, Danny, 59
Bradshaw, Terry, 15, 190, 208,
   225, 235
Brady, Dave, 232
Brady, John T., 210

Branch, Cliff, 73
Brandt, Gil, 131, 204
Breen, John, 21
Bregel, Jeff, 119
Brennan, Bud, 88
Breslin, Jimmy, 97
Brickhouse, Jack, 43, 221, 236
Briggs, Joe Bob (John Bloom), 106, 134
Brodie, John, 117, 136, 189
Brondfield, Jerry, 36, 105
Brookshier, Tom, 90, 94, 136, 173, 238
Brown, Jerome, 60
Brown, Jim, 211, 212
Brown, Mack, 69, 112
Brown, Paul, 41, 250
Brown, Rita Mae, 100
Brown, Tim, 171
Browning, David, 151
Broyles, Frank, 153
Bruce, Earle, 68, 95
Bruce, Gail, 217
Bruenig, Bob, 82
Bruno, Frank, 181
Bryan, Jimmy, 70
Bryant, Anita, 190
Bryant, Bear, 30, 33, 34, 35, 51, 52, 56, 65, 90, 91, 199, 243, 247
Buchwald, Art, 151
Buckley, William F., 198
Buehler, George, 78
Bullough, Hank, 19
Burns, Jerry, 181, 246
Burns, Leon, 213
Busey, Gary, 33
Butkus, Dick, 15, 43, 117, 119, 133, 169, 201, 225
Butz, Dave, 40
Byrne, Jim, 112

Caen, Herb, 129, 229
Callahan, Tom, 35
Camp, Walter, 81
Campbell, Earl, 18, 139, 207, 211, 213
Canadeo, Tony, 46
Cannon, Jimmy, 127
Carroll, Jerry, 197
Carson, Harry, 20, 117

Carson, Johnny, 55, 93, 128, 142
Casanova, Len, 37
Casem, Marino, 100
Casper, Dave, 139, 241
Cassady, Howard "Hopalong," 210
Cavanaugh, Matt, 115
Champi, Frank, 99
Chandler, Bob, 84
Chirkinian, Frank, 238
Chou En-lai, 127
Christensen, Todd, 84, 193
Christiani, Mike, 66
Clark, Dwight, 171, 197
Clark, Jessie, 211
Clark, Monte, 91, 213
Clemson, Danny Ford, 35
Clinkscale, Dexter, 169
Cogdill, Gail, 159
Cohn, Lowell, 39, 74, 145, 163, 216
Collins, Chuck, 186
Collinsworth, Cris, 253
Condon, Tom, 208
Connelly, Mike, 81
Connors, Cella Dupree, 82, 205
Connors, George "Moose," 221
Cook, Beano, 12, 58, 65, 86, 114, 197, 238
Coolidge, Calvin, 36
Cooper, Mark, 95
Corman, Avery, 143
Cornerly, Charley, 244
Corso, Lee, 12, 244
Coryell, Don, 40, 41
Cosbie, Doug, 19
Cosell, Howard, 91, 127, 129, 236, 237
Costas, Bob, 29, 47, 185, 240
Coury, Dick, 33
Cousineau, Tom, 83, 108, 119
Cowan, Charley, 155
Criqui, Don, 142
Crisler, Fritz, 87
Cronkite, Walter, 234
Cross, George L., 88
Cross, Randy, 19, 149, 150, 246
Crow, John David, 14, 183
Crowley, Jim, 63
Crutcher, Tommy Joe, 159, 249
Csonka, Larry, 86, 122, 211, 213

Cuniberti, Betty, 225
Cunningham, Randall, 191
Cunningham, Sam "The Bam,"
  214
Currie, Dan, 110
Curry, Bill, 124, 131, 139, 198,
  216, 219
Curry, Buddy, 120
Curtice, Jack, 210
Curtis, Mike, 120
Custer, George Armstrong, 13,
  246
Czarobski, Ziggy, 175

Dalton, William, 19
Dangerfield, Rodney, 12
Danielson, Gary, 169, 194, 222,
  238
Dasbach, Kurt, 58
Daugherty, Duffy, 14, 26, 85,
  175, 180, 204, 244, 247
Davidson, Ben, 135
Davis, Al, 121, 136, 141, 163,
  164, 181, 183, 184, 204, 246
Davis, Bill, 245
Davis, Mike, 108
Davis, Willie, 47
Day, Doris, 89
Dean, Fred, 77
Dean, James, 163
DeBartolo, Edward, Jr., 251
DeBerg, Steve, 191
DeLamielleure, Joe, 126
Dempsey, Jack, 13
Denton, Jeremiah, 56
DePalma, Steve, 63
De Pasqua, Carl, 52
Derek, Bo, 165
Devaney, Bob, 35, 51
Devine, Dan, 64
Dexter, Pete, 33, 48
Dickerson, Eric, 103, 124, 132,
  214
Dickey, Glenn, 65, 94, 200, 208
Dickey, Jim, 59, 118
Didinger, Ray, 156
Dieken, Doug, 75, 114, 155
Dierdorf, Dan, 13, 40, 111, 130,
  207
Diliberto, Buddy, 165
Ditka, Mike, 41, 43, 109, 196, 239

Dobie, Gil, 203
Dobler, Conrad, 16, 22, 28, 95,
  108, 113, 147, 154, 156, 169,
  184, 199, 200, 218
Dodd, Bobby, 25
Dodds, Deloss, 35
Doherty, Ed, 208
Donahue, Terry, 62, 204
Donlan, Jack, 114
Donovan, Art, 49, 109, 125, 126,
  132, 157, 166
Dorsett, Tony, 37, 213, 214
Doughty, Glenn, 167
Douglass, Bobby, 15
Downey, Mike, 12, 133, 137, 140,
  141, 145, 149, 195, 231
Dry, F. A., 214
DuBose, Doug, 118
Duhe, A. J., 168
Dupree, Marcus, 38, 82, 205
Durbin, Tom, 185

Edes, Gordon, 150
Edison, Thomas, 110
Edwards, Harry, 53
Edwards, LaVell, 11, 67, 105
Egierski, Walt, 35
Eisenhower, Dwight D., 17, 92
Ellerbee, Linda, 230
Elliott, John, 243
Elliott, Pete, 11
Elway, John, 32, 91, 137, 191,
  192, 236
Emerson, Ralph Waldo, 91
Emrich, Clyde, 218
Enberg, Dick, 20, 158
Erber, Lew, 16
Erhardt, Ron, 173
Evans, Bobbie, 167
Evans, Linda, 64
Evans, Norm, 102, 167, 241
Evashevski, Forrest, 93, 210
Everett, Jim, 192
Ewbank, Weeb, 42, 89, 162, 219
Exley, Frederick, 129, 190

Facenda, John, 99
Fairbanks, Chuck, 220
Falls, Joe, 36
Fambrough, Dan, 241
Faust, Gerry, 35

Felser, Larry, 17
Ferguson, Howie, 215
Ferguson, Joe, 192
Ferkany, Ed, 105
Fields, Andy, 82
Finks, Jim, 38
Flores, Tom, 42, 111
Flutie, Doug, 192
Foley, Tim, 168, 181
Ford, Danny, 35
Ford, Gerald R., 152
Foreman, Chuck, 211
Fortune, Hosea, 103
Foss, Joe, 88
Fourcade, John, 193
Fouts, Dan, 41, 85, 172
Fralic, Bill, Jr., 54
Fralic, Bill, Sr., 54
Francis, James, 118
Francis, Russ, 95, 170
Freeman, Tom, 153
Frei, Terri, 239
Friedman, Dick, 29
Friedman, Robert, 129
Fritsch, Toni, 81, 221
Fry, Hayden, 105
Fugett, Jean, 194
Fuller, Patrick, 237
Fuller, Steve, 102

Galat, Joe, 75
Gallagher, Jack, 47
Gallico, Paul, 96, 209
Garagiola, Joe, 230
Garrett, Alvin, 91
Garrett, Mike, 215
Garrison, Walt, 45, 215
Garvey, Ed, 115
Gastineau, Lisa, 77
Gastineau, Mark, 77
Gent, Peter, 44, 47, 111, 181,
   202, 228, 245
George, Phyllis, 237
George, Ray, 61
Gergen, Joe, 60, 65
Gibbs, Joe, 91
Gibron, Abe, 42
Gifford, Frank, 97, 128, 129, 195,
   215
Gilchrist, Cookie, 110
Gill, Turner, 94

Gillman, Sid, 21, 22, 215
Gilmer, Harry, 21
Gilmore, Tom, 240
Gipp, George, 87, 247
Glanville, Jerry, 34, 50, 86, 254
Glassic, Tom, 152
Glazer, Richard, 131
Golic, Bob, 168, 192
Gonzaga, John, 76
Gordon, Ira, 167
Gottfried, Mike, 59, 62
Graham, Billy, 227
Graham, Doug, 133
Graham, Julee, 30
Graham, Otto, 217
Grange, Red, 84, 126, 206, 212
Grant, Bud, 42, 43, 77, 129, 143,
   144, 177
Grantham, Larry, 110
Gray, Mel, 171
Green, Cornell, 250
Green, Hugh, 120
Green, Roy, 73
Greene, Bob, 215
Greene, "Mean Joe," 77, 108,
   130, 147, 189, 200, 227
Greenwood, L. C., 147, 231
Gregg, Barbara, 46
Gregg, Forrest, 46, 138
Griese, Bob, 32, 232, 241
Guest, Larry, 225
Gumbel, Bryant, 57

Hackman, Gene, 98
Haden, Pat, 23, 77, 80, 94, 143,
   193
Halas, George, 26, 39, 43, 44, 93,
   206, 221, 224
Hall, John, 52
Hampton, Dan, 79, 134
Hanifan, Jim, 147
Hannah, Charley, 42
Hannah, John, 156
Hannah, John A., 50
Hannah, Page, 156
Harmon, Tom, 28, 88, 210
Harper, Bruce, 131
Harrah, Dennis, 126, 154
Harris, Arne, 147
Harris, Bill, 62
Harris, Franco, 149, 208, 211, 216

Harvey, Steve, 58, 60, 61, 143, 150
Hauss, Len, 122
Hawkins, Alex, 89, 110
Hawkins, "Screamin' " Jay, 79
Hayes, Anne, 31, 249
Hayes, Bob, 172
Hayes, Lester, 72, 73, 142, 191
Hayes, Woody, 24, 25, 26, 31, 36, 52, 64, 90, 105, 107, 108, 180, 206, 210, 226, 244, 249
Haynes, Abner, 167
Hazeltine, Matt, 250
Heffelfinger, W. W. "Pudge," 84, 96, 106
Hein, Mel, 156
Heinsohn, Tom, 101
Heisman, John W., 25, 174, 175, 240
Henderson, Thomas "Hollywood," 22, 41, 45, 55, 112, 120, 172, 181, 190, 217
Hendricks, Ted, 121, 140, 141
Henning, Dan, 33
Henry, Orville, 38
Herman, Dave, 80, 250
Hermosillo, Xavier, 92
Herskowitz, Mickey, 217
Herzog, Ladd, 82
Hickey, Red, 44
Hilgenberg, Jay, 100, 154
Hill, Calvin, 119
Hill, Tony, 172
Hirsch, Elroy "Crazy Legs," 170, 172, 178, 251
Hoffa, Jimmy, 143
Holmes, Ernie, 147, 233
Holtz, Lou, 16, 19, 24, 26, 37, 54, 56, 61, 64, 65, 71, 83, 92, 95, 160, 171, 178, 182, 211, 226, 245, 253, 254
Holub, E. J., 167
Hooker, Fair, 172
Hooks, Roland, 222
Hoover, J. Edgar, 198
Hornung, Paul, 68, 143, 216, 249, 254
Howard, Frank, 34, 57
Howard, Jimmy, 35
Hubbard, Elbert, 50
Hubbard, Marv, 160

Huff, Sam, 116, 121, 145
Huffman, David, 155
Hughes, Howard, 208
Humphrey, Claude, 78, 242
Humphrey, Sandra, 78
Hunt, H. L., 165
Hunt, Lamar, 114, 164, 165
Hutchins, Robert Maynard, 50
Hutton, E. F., 12
Hyland, Bob, 157
Hyman, Mervin D., 36, 90

Irsay, Robert, 91, 193

Jackson, Charles, 115
Jackson, Earnest, 216
Jackson, Keith, 240
Jackson, Tom, 121
Jacobson, Mark, 79
James, Don, 205, 253
James, Lionel, 212
Jaworski, Ron, 142
Jefferson, John, 172
Jenkins, Dan, 36, 54, 63, 64, 66, 69, 104, 117, 136, 146, 162, 190, 224, 244, 247, 252
Jenkins, Ray, 61
Jennings, Dave, 221
Jimmy the Greek, 116, 239
Johnson, Cecil, 118, 122
Johnson, Jimmy, 37
Johnson, Lyndon B., 153
Johnson, Magic, 172
Johnson, Pete, 216
Jones, Bert, 193
Jones, Charlie, 160, 192, 212
Jones, Deacon, 107, 221
Jones, Earl, 17
Jones, Ed "Too Tall," 78, 103
Jones, Harry, 214
Jones, Stan, 43
Jones, T. A. D., 175
Jordan, Henry, 46, 157, 176
Jordan, Le Roy, 97, 122
Jostes, Randy, 185
Jurgensen, Sonny, 111, 188, 193

Kahn, Roger, 187, 229
Kapp, Joe, 11, 28, 43, 47, 68, 247
Karlis, Rich, 223, 242

Karras, Alex, 16, 17, 27, 74, 76, 79, 130, 133, 142, 155, 156, 159, 172, 176, 188, 193, 194, 198, 210, 215, 218, 221, 241, 248
Keating, Tom, 75, 135, 147
Kelcher, Louie, 78
Kellner, Jenny, 194
Kelly, Emmett, 215
Kelly, Jim, 133
Kennedy, Jayne, 237
Kennedy, John F., 97
Kerbawy, Nick, 130
Khomeini, Ayatollah Ruhollah, 202
Kiick, Jim, 86
Kilmer, Billy, 90, 188
Kiner, Steve, 70
King, Gordon, 114
King, Kenny, 211, 212
King, Larry, 128
King, Peter H., 228
Klecko, Joe, 78
Klein, Gene, 34, 41, 48, 77, 78, 113, 115, 128, 148, 149, 162, 164, 165, 166, 183, 209, 213, 223
Klein, Robert, 236, 237
Klosterman, Don, 201
Knight, Tuffy, 95
Knox, Chuck, 44, 177
Koch, Greg, 138
Kornheiser, Tony, 80, 146, 214, 239
Kosar, Bernie, 135, 194
Kotcheff, Ted, 111
Kozlowski, Glen, 13, 57, 253
Kramer, Jerry, 46, 79, 101, 123, 159
Kramer, Tommy, 66, 111, 194
Krieg, Dave, 194
Kristynik, Marvin, 123
Kuechenberg, Bob, 234
Kuharich, Joe, 244
Kurtis, Bill, 148
Kush, Frank, 139, 251
Kwiatkowski, Mickey, 59

Lacewell, Larry, 70
Lambert, Jack, 112, 122, 136
Lamm, Richard, 90

Lammons, Pete, 232
Lamonica, Daryle, 188
Landry, Tom, 33, 42, 44, 45, 90, 171, 178, 197, 221, 233, 241, 245
Lane, Dick "Night Train," 71, 107, 124
Lanier, Willie, 122
Lardner, Ring, 39
Largent, Steve, 173, 209
Lavery, Dennis, 57
Lawrence, Henry, 157, 246
Layden, Elmer, 38, 63
Layne, Bobby, 110, 137, 194, 195, 204, 246
Leahy, Frank, 88, 175
Lee, Bill, 67, 73
Lemons, Abe, 102
Leno, Jay, 113
Letterman, David, 100, 109, 115, 116, 146, 185, 186, 235, 239
Levy, Marv, 66, 115
Lewis, D. D., 135, 147, 216
Lewis, Jerry, 184
Lewis, Tommy, 88
Ley, Bob, 67
Lindblom, John, 43
Linderman, Larry, 52
Lindsay, John V., 89
Lipscomb, Gene "Big Daddy," 74, 79, 107
LoCosale, Al, 28
Lofton, James, 171
Logan, Dave, 122
Lomax, Neil, 195, 239
Lombardi, Harry, 166
Lombardi, Marie, 159
Lombardi, Vince, 20, 39, 45, 46, 47, 52, 81, 97, 125, 131, 138, 157, 159, 166, 175, 176, 180, 210, 216, 231, 236, 248
Long, Bob, 173
Long, Howie, 109, 136
Looney, Douglas, S., 32, 35, 37, 38, 191
Looney, Joe Don, 14, 15, 20, 21, 166, 210, 216
Luciano, Ron, 144
Lujack, Johnny, 88
Lynch, Dan, 106
Lyons, Marty, 77

McAtee, Harvey, 153
McCafferty, Don, 120
McCallum, Jack, 62
McCallum, John D., 39
McCarthy, Eugene, 101
McCartney, Bill, 72
McCarver, Tim, 148
McConkey, Phil, 173
McCord, Gary, 148
McCormack, Mike, 224
McDonald, Paul, 155
McDonough, John, 221
McElhenny, Hugh, 205, 217
McElroy, Vann, 85
McGee, Max, 30, 109, 173, 231, 248, 254
McGrath, John, 230
McInally, Pat, 222
McKay, John, 34, 37, 38, 40, 86, 98, 104, 106, 138, 150, 156, 162, 177, 201, 214, 220, 237, 245, 247
McKinney, Dump, 252
Mackovic, John, 179
McLean, Ron, 57
McLuhan, Marshall, 99
McMahon, Jim, 104, 154, 196, 202, 235
McMahon, Roberta, 196
McNally, Johnny "Blood," 47
McWilliams, David, 69
Madden, John, 18, 23, 26, 28, 55, 78, 83, 86, 117, 126, 127, 140, 145, 157, 158, 164, 171, 173, 180, 182, 189, 193, 196, 202, 207, 223, 230, 239, 246
Madden, Michael, 144
Madro, Joe, 152
Maguire, Paul, 155
Mailer, Norman, 85
Majors, Johnny, 37
Mandarich, Tony, 38
Mandell, Arnold J., 21
Manilow, Barry, 231
Manley, Dexter, 153
Mann, Carol, 48
Manning, Archie, 17, 23, 114, 195, 208
Mano, D. Keith, 58
Mansfield, Ray, 212
Marino, Dan, 143

Marshall, George Preston, 212
Marshall, Jim, 201
Martha, Paul, 185
Martilotta, Jack, 75
Martin, Abe, 22, 83
Martin, Doug, 78
Martin, Harvey, 120, 136, 252
Martin, Rod, 122
Martz, Ron, 134
Mason, Tony, 11
Matte, Tom, 216
Matuszak, John "The Tooz", 27, 41, 79, 86, 108, 112, 121, 141, 163, 182, 190, 234, 251
Mauck, Carl, 198
Maule, Tex, 232
Maxwell, Tiny, 151
Mazur, Johnny, 47
Mecklenburg, Karl, 121, 123
Mecom, John, 161, 165
Merchant, Larry, 98, 127, 198, 227
Meredith, Don, 42, 45, 67, 99, 128, 129, 130, 180, 188, 195, 197, 215
Metcalf, Terry, 217
Meyer, Ron, 153, 182
Michaels, Al, 130
Michaels, Walt, 222
Miklasz, Bernie, 236
Millard, Bryan, 124, 154
Millard, Connie, 154
Millen, Matt, 123
Miller, Arthur, 187
Miller, Bill, 60
Miller, Don, 63
Miller, Ira, 227
Mills, Chuck, 93, 176
Mitchell, Suzanne, 29
Modell, Art, 135, 148, 184
Moen, Kevin, 91
Montana, Joe, 197, 199
Montville, Leigh, 84
Moody, Fred, 119, 150, 194
Moore, Derland, 242
Moore, Myrel, 123
Moore, Tom, 23
Morella, Joe, 248
Morgan, Stanley, 173
Morrall, Earl, 81
Morris, Joe, 217

Morris, Willie, 99
Morrison, Joe, 18
Morrow, Jeff, 167
Morton, Craig, 138
Moseley, Mark, 229
Motley, Marion, 217
Mount, Anson, 144
Mozart, Wolfgang Amadeus, 49
Muir, Bill, 152
Muncie, Chuck, 217, 218
Murchison, Clint, 186
Murphy, Austin, 118
Murray, Eddie, 222
Murray, Jim, 13, 14, 36, 41, 44,
  49, 51, 75, 79, 125, 127, 142,
  155, 156, 172, 195, 203, 215,
  227
Musburger, Brent, 116, 230
Musick, Phil, 148
Myers, Jim, 81

Nader, Ralph, 228
Nagurski, Bronko, 61, 125, 218
Namath, Joe, 25, 56, 73, 89, 110,
  111, 159, 189, 197, 198, 224,
  232, 249
Nantz, Jim, 37
Navratilova, Martina, 138
Nehemiah, Renaldo, 109, 173
Nelson, Darrin, 218
Nelson, Lindsey, 23, 191
Nevius, C. W., 100
Newhart, Bob, 210
Newton, Nate, 82
Nielsen, Gifford, 198
Nietzsche, Friedrich, 36
Nitschke, Jackie, 249
Nitschke, Ray, 107, 110, 117,
  123, 176, 249
Nixon, Richard M., 36, 46, 93,
  96, 151, 184, 187, 188, 232
Nobis, Tommy, 116, 123
Noll, Chuck, 16, 47, 85, 108, 244
Nolte, Nick, 111
Norris, Rex, 62
Nugent, Tom, 197

Oliver, Chip, 110
Olsen, Merlin, 79, 81, 156, 200
Osmond family, 56
Ostler, Scott, 42, 143, 234, 239

Owen, John, 196
Owen, Steve, 96, 206, 218
Ozzie and Harriet, 164

Paciorek, Tom, 243
Page, Alan, 229
Papanek, John, 144
Parcells, Bill, 120, 252
Paris, Bubba, 49
Parker, Buddy, 88
Parker, Jim, 157
Parrish, Bernie, 161
Parrish, Stan, 24, 92, 246
Parton, Dolly, 212
Pastorini, Dan, 94, 188, 198
Paterno, Joe, 93, 176
Payton, Eddie, 114
Payton, Walter, 212, 218
Peale, Norman Vincent, 12, 229
Pell, Charlie, 176
Perkins, Mike, 31
Perkins, Ray, 31, 140, 185, 252
Perkins, Steve, 197
Perles, George, 53, 103
Perry, William "The Refrigerator,"
  79, 80, 82
Peterson, Bill, 89
Philipp, Harold, 105
Phillips, Bum, 12, 19, 21, 23, 26,
  27, 31, 33, 47, 48, 49, 54, 76,
  77, 82, 85, 111, 131, 132, 139,
  144, 145, 161, 170, 179, 181,
  182, 207, 213, 217, 226, 242,
  250, 251, 253
Phillips, Gary, 220
Phillips, Helen, 250, 253, 254
Phillips, William, 97
Plank, Doug, 109, 119, 207, 213
Plimpton, George, 83, 89, 105,
  174, 251
Plum, Milt, 21, 198
Pollom, Norm, 223
Povich, Shirley, 212
Powers, Francis, 172
Pritzker, A. N., 165
Proctor, Mel, 71
Prothro, Tommy, 177
Prowse, Juliet, 30

Quayle, Dan, 20

Ralston, John, 27, 93
Ramos, Frank, 232
Rappold, Kyle, 100, 169
Rashad, Ahmad, 17, 32, 65, 114, 117, 122, 153, 167, 174, 183, 214, 240, 242
Raveling, George, 67, 102
Reagan, Ronald W., 102
Redford, Robert, 228
Reeves, Dan, 32, 39, 40, 137
Reid, Mike, 80
Reid, Tim, 146
Reinert, Al, 98
Retting, Tony, 72
Revere, Paul, 152
Reynolds, Jack, 117
Rice, Grantland, 63, 125
Rice, Jerry, 174
Rice, Tony, 254
Rickles, Don, 44
Riegels, Roy "Wrong Way," 14
Riggins, John, 18, 112, 131, 168, 207, 218, 230, 234
Robbie, Joe, 113, 165
Roberts, Larry, 179
Robertson, John, 186
Robertson, Sam, 178
Robinson, Dave, 123
Robinson, Eddie, 52, 90
Robinson, Jerry, 112
Robinson, John, 115, 192, 218
Robinson, Mark, 72
Robustelli, Andy, 145
Rockne, Knute, 14, 24, 25, 38, 71, 87, 92, 179, 209, 220, 243
Roder, Mirro, 133
Rodgers, Johnny, 184
Rodgers, Pepper, 32, 203, 205
Rodriquez, Ruben, 224
Rogers, Darryl, 64, 173
Rogers, Don, 73
Rogers, Will, 12, 15, 38, 249
Rohrer, Jeff, 71
Rooney, Andy, 230
Rooney, Art, 47, 147, 161
Rooney, Art, Jr., 118
Roosevelt, Eleanor, 25
Roosevelt, Theodore, 106
Rosenberg, Howard, 237
Rosenbloom, Carroll, 31, 161, 166
Rosenthal, David N., 229

Rosenthal, Harold, 48
Rossovich, Tim, 16
Rothrock, Jack, 60
Royal, Darrell, 25, 30, 31, 55
Royko, Mike, 80, 237
Rozelle, Pete, 28, 110, 184, 238
Ruby, Michael, 228
Rutigliano, Sam, 73, 119, 163, 199
Ruzich, Dan, 118
Ryan, Buddy, 147, 154, 174, 216, 224
Rypien, Mark, 20

Sabol, Steve, 235
Salem, Tim, 63
Sample, Johnny, 42
Sanders, Barry, 104, 132, 219
Sanders, Charlie, 238
Sanders, Red, 15, 243
Sauer, George, 170, 216
Saunders, Al, 48
Sayers, Gale, 211, 219
Schembechler, Bo, 13, 206, 226, 245, 254
Schlichter, Art, 189
Schmidt, Joe, 126, 175
Schonewise, Quintin 54
Schottenheimer, Marty, 18
Schrader, Loel, 141
Schramm, Tex, 86
Schuh, Henry, 157
Schwartzwalder, Ben, 30
Scott, Bobby, 199
Scott, Jake, 89
Seals, Leon "Dr. Sack," 115
Secretariat, 112
Seifert, George, 179
Selmon, Lee Roy, 80
Septien, Raphael, 223
Shapiro, Harold, 54
Sharp, Alan, 98
Shaughnessy, Clark, 87
Shaw, Bill, 69
Shaw, Irwin, 200
Shaw, Pete, 174
Shecter, Leonard, 241
Sheeley, Glenn, 248
Shell, Art, 158
Shelton, Gary, 95
Sherman, Allie, 48, 187, 247

Sherrard, Mike, 252
Sherrill, Jackie, 20
Sherrod, Blackie, 74
Shinnick, Don, 124
Shofner, Del, 174
Shofner, Jim, 38
Shoor, Lonnie, 125
Shula, Don, 42, 48, 49, 232
Shula, Dorothy, 48
Simers, T. J., 48
Simmons, Edwin, 168
Simmons, Lon, 44, 199
Simpson, O. J., 130, 211, 219, 220
Sims, Billy, 38
Sims, Gerald, 204
Sinkwich, Frank, 240
Sipe, Brian, 22, 134, 199
Sistrunk, Otis, 130
Sizemore, Jerry, 153
Skoronski, Bob, 45
Sloan, Steve, 70
Smerlas, Fred, 84
Smith, Bubba, 206, 247
Smith, Don, 21
Smith, Gary, 138, 164, 202, 220
Smith, Homer, 252
Smith, Julian, 53
Smith, Red, 46, 127, 137
Snyder, Bill, 179
Sons, Ray, 44
Sortum, Rick, 177
Spahn, Warren, 101
Spander, Art, 184, 185, 223
Spurrier, Steve, 199
Stabler, Ken, 24, 26, 83, 111, 131, 141, 157, 163, 188, 189, 198, 199, 200, 207, 208, 209, 242, 250
Stagg, Amos Alonzo, 39
Stallings, Gene, 240
Staples, Jack, 11
Starkey, Joe, 91
Starr, Bart, 46, 49
Staubach, Roger, 25, 172, 200, 202
Stautner, Ernie, 78
Steadman, John, 140
Steinbeck, John, 65
Steinbrenner, George, 165
Stickles, Monty, 64

Stillwell, Roger, 29
Stolle, Cal, 62
Stoner, Neale, 59
Stoudt, Cliff, 131, 189
Stovall, Jerry, 62
Stram, Hank, 167, 180, 195
Streep, Meryl, 145
Streisand, Barbra, 30
Stuhldreher, Harry, 63
Sullivan, John L., 101
Summerall, Pat, 23, 237, 238
Svare, Harland, 48, 161
Swann, Lynn, 73, 125
Swilley, Dennis, 194
Switzer, Barry, 15, 33, 38, 65, 219

Tarkenton, Fran, 94, 145, 187, 200, 250
Tatum, Jack, 108
Taylor, Jimmy, 121, 131, 215
Taylor, Lawrence, 55, 115, 117, 120, 124, 183, 235
Teaff, Grant, 68
Teller, Edward, 98
Testaverde, Vinny, 65, 140
Theismann, Joe, 74, 169, 189, 196
Thiel, Art, 13
Thielemann, R. C., 252
Thomas, Duane, 227
Thomas, Russ, 186
Thompson, Hunter S., 42, 46, 93, 97, 125, 128, 140, 163, 164, 170, 219
Thorpe, Jim, 220
Tierney, Tim, 245
Tikonov, Viktor, 98
Tiller, Shake, 224
Tiny Tim, 232
Tittle, Y. A., 101, 107, 123, 145, 190, 200
Todd, Doug, 233
Tomczak, Mike, 192
Toomay, Pat, 155
Tose, Leonard, 166
Traynowicz, Mark, 253
Truman, Harry S., 17, 30
Trumpy, Bob, 171
Tubbs, Billy, 97
Tucker, Arnold, 88

Tunney, Gene, 13
Turner, Bulldog, 125, 221
Tutko, Thomas, 29
Twain, Mark, 197
Twilley, Howard, 207
Tyler, Wendell, 220

Uecker, Bob, 169
Underwood, John, 22, 165
Unitas, Johnny, 125, 127, 187, 200, 201
Upshaw, Gene, 141, 148, 152, 158, 221

Valdiserri, Roger, 219
Van Allen, James, 51
Van Brocklin, Norm, 49, 188, 201, 226
Van Horne, Keith, 133
Van Note, Jeff, 209
Verdi, Bob, 134
Vermeil, Dick, 234

Waggoner, Glen, 79, 139, 164, 229
Walden, Jim, 57, 70, 92
Walker, Doak, 127, 194, 225
Walker, Herschel, 182, 185, 220, 225
Walker, Johnny, 60
Walker, Wayne, 107, 197
Wallace, George, 35
Wallace, William N., 89
Walsh, Bill, 49, 50, 178, 191, 211, 220, 228
Walters, Stan, 76, 153
Ward, Chris, 158
Ward, Robert, 165
Warmath, Murray, 51
Warner, Pop, 39, 87
Washington, Anthony, 74
Waterfield, Bob, 201
Waters, Charlie, 72, 74, 168
Watson, Glenn, 17
Watts, Ted, 222
Wayne, John, 197, 232
Weaver, Phil, Jr., 124
Welch, Raquel, 45
Welk, Lawrence, 71
Whicker, Mark, 217
White, Danny, 202, 214, 223
White, Dwight, 147

White, Gordon S., Jr., 36, 90
White, Mike, 178
White, Randy, 80, 131
Whittaker, Jack, 150
Wiggin, Paul, 39, 53, 218
Wilbur, John, 135
Wiley, Ralph, 147, 191
Wilkinson, Bud, 88
Will, George F., 33, 100
Williams, Doug, 202
Williams, Edward Bennett, 40, 163
Williams, Henry, 174
Williams, Robin, 72
Williamson, Fred "The Hammer," 231
Wilson, Marc, 202, 203
Winslow, Kellen, 85, 103, 160, 174
Winston, Dennis, 132
Wood, Bob, 89
Woodside, Woody, 182
Woolford, Donnell, 74
Wooten, Ron, 235
Wright, Orville, 43
Wright, Steve, 186
Wyche, Sam, 45, 134, 135, 183, 233
Wyman, Mike, 69
Wynne, Cera, 99
Wysocki, Pete, 213

Yablans, Frank, 111
Yeoman, Bill, 17
Yost, Fielding, 20, 39, 243
Young, Bob, 158
Young, Dick, 49
Young, Fredd, 124
Young, Rickey, 22
Youngblood, Jack, 117, 233
Yount, Robin, 103

Zamberletti, Fred, 167
Zappa, Frank, 28
Zendejas, Alan, 243
Zendejas, Luis, 224
Ziegler, Brent, 205
Zimmerman, Paul, 50, 113, 120, 137, 146, 154, 191, 202
Zuppke, Bob, 50, 92, 107, 151, 179, 203, 224, 243

ABOUT THE AUTHORS

Bob Chieger is the editor of the *Northwest Examiner*, a newspaper in Portland, Oregon. He is the author of five books, including three on sports. He has won awards in investigative reporting and business writing. He is single and lives in Portland.

Pat Sullivan is a sportswriter for the *San Francisco Chronicle* where he covers golf and pro football. He lives with his wife and two children in San Rafael, California. This is the second book on which the authors have collaborated.